BRS
THE EARLY YEARS
1948-1953

BRITISH ROAD SERVICES

First published in 1999 by
Roundoak Publishing
The Old Dairy, Perry Farm, East Nynehead,
Wellington, Somerset TA21 ODA

Tel. 01823 461997   Fax 01823 461998
email: roundoak@netcomuk.co.uk

ISBN 1 871565 33 2

Design by Peter Davies

Origination by Roundoak Associates

Printed in Great Britain by
The Amadeus Press, Huddersfield

ACKNOWLEDGEMENTS

The main supporter of this volume has been my
good friend Gordon Mustoe who, with his excellent
Fisher Renwick story behind him, has given freely of
his time and knowledge in providing a large part of
the story. In addition he has drawn up the extensive
supplement detailing the BRS groups etc.

Much of the "fine detail" regarding individual
vehicles, depots, groups and fleets came from the
memory and records of BRS expert Mike Houle, a
friend since the 1950s.

I am also indebted to friends Alan B. Cross, Andy
Ping, Jim Wyndham and Bill Godwin for the use of
photographs and information as requested, but
particular tribute must be made to the late Philip
Hine. It was he who had the foresight to tour various
parts of the country in order to make a photographic
record of many of the vehicles operated by
independent hauliers, in that important period when
the BTC was acquiring companies. This is the first
time that the majority of these photographs have
been published - and what an important record they
make.

A few of the photographs came from the collection
of the late Ted Oates, a friend of many years who had
a particular interest in some of the pre-nationalisation
fleets, such as Fisher Renwick and Youngs Express
Deliveries. His memory lives on in the Scammell
Rigid 8 of Young's, which he so well restored.

I have also used a few photographs taken from
BRS sources, for which I am grateful. Many of the
other photos come from my own roadside collection,
some of which have appeared in earlier publications,
including Truck Nostalgia (Blandford Press), and the
1953 edition of ABC British Road Services (Ian Allan).

The information concerning vehicles, companies,
BRS groups and dates which has gone into the photo
captions has come from many sources. Fleet notes
from enthusiasts, references from Commercial Motor,
but most importantly information obtained from the
Public Record Office, Kew (PRO). The Lists of
Acquired Undertakings and the BRS Gazetteer also
provide useful information on the early days of the
organisation as it progressed into maturity.

The papers of Quick Smith and Dunbar, held at
the Modern Records Centre, University of Warwick,
also yielded valuable information and detail, and
saved countless hours of research elsewhere.

BRS
THE EARLY YEARS
1948-1953

**Arthur Ingram
and
Gordon Mustoe**

An account of the origins and
growth of Britain's nationalised
road transport system,
fifty years on

ROUNDOAK PUBLISHING

AUTHOR'S PREFACE

The idea of producing a book dealing with the history of British Road Services has been with me for a long time, but I have always felt that the subject is so vast, that several volumes would be needed.

So with the 50 year anniversary coming about, I thought it appropriate to at least take a look at the very beginnings of that important era in our transport history. I also felt it an opportune moment to put into print, some details of those individuals and companies who all went together to create the nationalised giant.

Readers will find that I have dealt at some length with our road transport operators of the pre-nationalisation period, for it was they who did all the graft in creating the industry. All the British Transport Commission did was to attempt to weld it together with the law protecting them, and without the need to prove their place in the industry by way of competition and licensing.

Most readers will be aware of how the BTC and BRS came about, by way of the huge swing toward socialisation in the aftermath of the 1939-1945 war.

The great surge forward of road transport during the 1920s, gave rise to many pieces of legislation framed to control the numerous individuals who saw the tremendous potential within their grasp. These individuals ranged from the lowly man with a horse-and-cart, right through to more acute entrepreneurs who were anxious to corner as much of the market as possible for themselves.

Amongst all this melee of operators, legislation, vehicles and competition, were the many thousands of employed drivers. It was they who helped turn the undercurrent of social unrest in the old system, into the great tide which swept the new concept into being.

Many of them could see a new beginning, with a greater emphasis on the welfare of the workers. No long hours, no more dodgy nights out, no lack of vehicle maintenance. The promise of better wages and conditions, modern depot facilities, trade union recognition, and above all the abolition of competition which caused so many of the smaller operators to operate at cut rates, which in turn created a necessity to reduce operating costs.

So, in 1948 the future looked bright for the new transport controllers, they having high hopes for an all-embracing system of transport with the emphasis on integration.

The Grand Plan swung into action on 1st July 1948 when the Regulations came into force detailing that the Notices of Acquisition must be served on road transport operators during the fifteen month period between 1st October 1948 and 1st January 1950.

Right: At the time of nationalisation the James Sutherland of Peterhead fleet stood at some 96 vehicles and it formed the basis for the Peterhead-Fraserburgh group, which in 1950 totalled 165 units engaged on general haulage and fish traffic. Pictured in the Peterhead depot is an AEC 'Mammoth Major' - fresh in its first coat of red - standing alongside a postwar 'Beaver' which retains the old Sutherland livery.

INTRODUCTION

Although British Road Services ceased to exist as such around 50 years after it had been created, there seems to be a continuing interest in the activities of the organisation. Any literature published by BRS or about BRS is fast becoming collectable, photographs of their vehicles are sought after, and an increasing number of preserved vehicles appear in their colours.

For some people within the transport industry, the very creation of BRS rendered them without a business. Others were able to get out of the industry, at a time that suited them. To many employees, it seemed like a gift from heaven.

To the enthusiast, not that there were many of them, it was a chance to study the fleet no matter where you went in the country. The acquisitions were not shrouded in secrecy, the depot staff were usually helpful, and here was a chance to record a major portion of the country's transport units.

In this book we take a look at the creation of that vast fleet during its formative period, before the change of government in 1952 put the whole procedure on hold, and eventually reverse the nationalisation machine. Much of the information concerns the general haulage side of the BTC business. Pickfords already been studied in a previous book, and little is made of parcels and meat cartage, both of which deserve separate study, with individual publications to come later.

CONTENTS

The Pioneering Years 1948-1953

The end of the Great War on 11th November 1918 left a run-down railway system, with both the Companies and railwaymen feeling betrayed by the Government.

The policy of a weak Ministry of Transport (MoT) with Lord Geddes as its first Minister together with the creation of the four grouped companies; the G.W.R., L.M.&S.R., L.&N.E.R., and the S.R. from the 130 existing railway companies, rather than their nationalisation, did little to prepare them to deal with the increasing competition from new expanding road transport firms.

Road transport was now taking, and retaining ever more of the profitable traffic from the railways, this unwittingly being helped by the rail strikes of 1919, 1924 and particularly that of 1926, which with miners strikes, enabled road transport to demonstrate that the railways were now an alternative, rather than the only commercial way to distribute goods.

Both the MoT and the railways were becoming concerned to restrict the competition from road. Royal Commissions and Committees were set up to look into the problem. At the grouping, the Railways were left with a complex rates tariff, based on 'what the traffic would bear', intended to produce a gross revenue which would cover/equal rails total costs plus a return on the capital.

The Institute of Transport, formed in 1921, at that time with little road representation, also sought an answer. Supply was exceeding demand with rate cutting becoming an accepted practice for general haulage, a lasting consequence being poor maintenance and unsafe vehicles, and harsh conditions for drivers, not helped by roads unchanged since the demise of the stage coach.

The 1928 Railway Road Powers Act enabled the railway companies to carry out their preferred choice of buying shares in existing road transport firms and bus companies. Some twenty firms were to be acquired, fully as with the Hays Wharf Group, or by acquiring half shareholdings as with Currie and Co., Wordie, and later Sutton & Co. (See Table 1, page 10). The Railways also had their own fleets of motor vehicles for collection and delivery, which even then were probably operating at a loss.

The 1930 Royal Commission on Transport report recognised the problem without suggesting any solution other than co-ordination with rail for long-distance trunking.

The 1933 Salter Report was intended to place the railways with their high fixed costs on an equal basis with road. Salter, a professional civil servant, carried out the brief to establish fair costs between the railways and road transport.
The principal recommendations in the report were incorporated in the Road Traffic Act 1933 to achieve this by:

1. Introducing the A. and B. licences for the carriage of goods for hire or reward, and C. licence for the carriage of goods by an 'own-account operator. The Railways could object to licences being granted.

2. Levying a new scale of charges for the Road Fund licence, with increased unladen and gross vehicle weight scales, with penalties for running on solid tyres.

3. The establishment of the Transport Advisory Council to advise and assist the MoT in relation to means of facilities for transport and their co-ordination.

Note: It was not until 1937 that the above Council made its recommendation that all forms of transport be rate controlled.

Whilst the railway rates were controlled by statute, this was not true in practice. The rate could be adjusted to prevent loss to road, as one way of co-ordination, and there were agreements for particular traffics. The parcels and smalls carriers were particularly affected by this.

There were no regulations to control the charges or rates for road transport, hence the successful public relations 'Fair Deal' campaign introduced by the railways in 1938, only to be ended with the outbreak of War.

Following the end of the Second World War, with the railways again run down, the Labour Party's solution in its manifesto was the nationalisation of all transport including railways and long distance road transport. Herbert Morrison - in his 'Socialisation of Transport 1932' - was the only politician who had given serious thought to the practicalities of how this could be done, considering it to be "most difficult and complicated".

The success of the Labour landslide saw Morrison's influence in the concept of the British Transport Commission (BTC) as a free standing enterprise run by businessmen of proven capability, without day to day Government interference.

A committee of the Traffic Commissioners had favoured hire and reward to be in three zones:

1. Journeys under 15-20 miles.
2. An intermediate zone.
3. Journeys over 20-40 miles.

The largest radius of the three was to be restricted to the proposed British Road Services (BRS) with exceptions for exempted traffics. (The recently ended Road Haulage Organisation (RHO) limit was 60 miles).

Own account or C licencees would be broadly free, with conditions as to conduct.

Roger Sewill for the newly formed Road Haulage Association (R.H.A.) expressed their concern at the proposed 25 mile limit, and wanted a committee of enquiry before any nationalisation Bill was presented. However, because they were unwilling to enter into any discussion with the Minister of Transport, Alfred Barnes, there was to be no consultation with the A and B licence part of the industry.

Barnes had wanted consultation as there was goodwill between the MoT and members of the industry who had worked as units of the RHO. However, Henry Dutfield - elected

5

as the RHA Chairman on 1st January 1945 - would not allow members to be told of this, and they carried out an intensive if ineffective anti-nationalisation campaign, including a film 'When the Wheels Slow Down'. Protest rallies were also held at major centres throughout the country, starting with the London rally in July 1947, sometimes resulting in mixed publicity. There were prosecutions for misuse of petrol, whilst Blackburn's rally resulted in W.H. Bowker and the local RHA secretary being charged with 'conducting a procession without previous notice', this infringing a Blackburn bye-law.

There were instances of where hauliers' customers voiced their uncertainties direct to the RTE, that their business must receive the same level of service under the new regime. If no commitment was received, then these customers would have no hesitation in resorting to the use of C-licensed fleets in order to maintain their expected level of service.

One particular case was that of the International Tea Stores, who were so concerned about the level of service provided by the Metropolitan Transport Supply Co. (a wholly owned subsidiary of the International Tea Stores), that it made known to the BTC that should no assurances be forthcoming, then they would not hesitate in creating a sizeable C-licence fleet under the name of Kearley & Tonge.

The manner in which some customers held their haulage contractors in such high regard, is borne out by reference to letters from the Dyestuffs Division of ICI, who regarded Lawtons Transport Ltd as the providers of their transport fleet. The whole of Lawtons' fleet was employed on ICI work, and the 60-odd vehicles was operated under A-contract licences to that company. Established very early in the century by John Thomas Lawton, the business handled traffic for the Broughton Copper Co. Ltd, which was acquired by ICI around 1934, and from 1939 the fleet was exclusively employed on work for this one customer.

The RHA claimed the Government should take hauliers into their confidence a little more; this despite their own attitude of no discussions with the MoT. G.W. Quick Smith, the then secretary and legal adviser of first the Road Transport Executive (RTE) and then, from October 1949, the Road Haulage Executive (RHE) was positive this rejection by the RHA was most adverse. Indeed on the Act receiving Royal Assent on 6th August 1947, Lord Woolton told Dutfield and Quick Smith 'to come to terms with reality', which they readily did, taking appointments with the RTE.

It is fortunate that on his retirement Quick Smith recorded his memoirs of BRS, providing an essential source for any history of the administration and development of BRS.

Among points raised during debates at the various stages were; there should be a limit of 50 miles, with a point to point distance of 80 miles. This was apparently based on a Road Haulage Wages Council definition of a short distance applying to a seven ton gross weight vehicle. It was also claimed that a 25 miles radius would limit the operating area to 1,900 square miles, whereas a 50 miles radius would quadruple the

operating area to some 8,000 square miles.

Concern for the Milk Marketing Board milk collections brought the response that only contract hauliers were used to carry their milk, and there would not be a problem. The Meat Pool vehicles were also said to be operating under contract.

Film Transport was said to have 58 operating companies using 300 vehicles for the delivery and exchange of films to some 4,600 cinemas. In the event the largest of these, F.T.S., were to be granted a three-year original permit.

It was also suggested that ownership was not necessary to control road transport. Instead of the acquisition of undertakings, they should be sub-contractors, with BRS acting as the National clearing house. Lord Llewelyn, who was involved in transport suggested "Clearing houses were recognised in the Bill, and BRS could deal with them as Agents". The RHA had a Clearing House section at this time.

Some of the RHE Board, including Quick Smith, were surprised at the amount of sub-contracting by the large companies. The firm of All British Carriers was quoted as up to 75% of the traffic being sub-contracted. No doubt Claude Barrington and his experiences with the Transport Services Group would have made all clear.

The proposed Act defined a long distance journey as being of 40 miles or more, during the course of which the vehicle was more than 25 miles from its operating centre. Permits would allow exemptions to cover greater distances. The 25-mile radius was to commence 1 July 1949. Own account C licencees were not to be restricted.

During the Committee stage of the Bill, the representations of the members in both chambers for Co-operatives (Barnes had been Chairman of the Co-operative Party, with at least 35 M.Ps sponsored by the Co-ops) and for the Federation of British Industries, together with other interests, were able to ensure that C Licencees were excluded. At the same time the radius for exemption was reduced to 25 miles. The exemption for C licences was to prove fundamental in preventing any successful attempt to bring about road and rail co-ordination.

Seven special categories of traffic were excluded: Bulk liquids; Explosives; Household Furniture, (including for a period new furniture); Meat (already controlled as part of the Meat Transport Organisation Limited (MTOL); Abnormal Indivisible loads; General Livestock (also already controlled by the MTOL); and Felled Timber.

The British Transport Commission had five executives: Road Transport, Railways, Docks and Inland Waterways, London Transport, and Hotels. The Road Transport Executive was subsequently divided into the Road Haulage and the Road Passenger Executive in June 1949.

The Road Transport Executive was required:

1. To compulsorily acquire predominantly long distance road haulage undertakings, compensating the owners according to the terms defined in the Act. The payment being made by British Transport Commission Stock.

2. It was also empowered to acquire by voluntary agreement any road haulage undertaking, (long distance or local). The intention was that these would be the sizeable limited companies, mostly former RHO Units. These undertakings would form the nucleus for BRS, and be 'lead' units for integrating the early compulsory acquisitions. Their compensation was negotiable, and would be paid in cash.

Left: The imposing St. Stephen's Tower (universally known as 'Big Ben') looks down on two ERFs of the old G.H. Atkins fleet, as they swing round Parliament Square en route eastwards along the Thames in 1950. G.H. Atkins & Sons were based near Rochester, Kent and operated about 20 vehicles. They were acquired by BRS early in 1949 and allocated as Unit A75, becoming part of 4A Medway group, which was later recoded upon transfer to South Western Division.

3. It could also be required to acquire whole or part of the long distance operations of a haulier if a permit was refused or revoked for any reason.

The five, soon to be six, Executives were statutory bodies, and the question of their responsibility was clear; they were to report to the Minister, not the Commission. This was a sensible decision when Parliament's interest could include:

Parliamentary Questions. These could and did cover any subject, sometimes even dealing with a constituents complaint over a late or damaged parcel.

A Debate, including that on the Commissions Annual Report, including that part devoted to the RHE.

Letters to M.Ps. (1,800 were received in 1950).

White Papers. The subject of a Select Committee - although the Executive was not to be chosen to a subject for inquiry during this period.

The BTC Headquarters Board representing BRS did meet with Parliament each month to discuss 'broad developments and account for their stewardship'.

The Commission retained responsibility for forming policies and direction of administration, delegating to the Executives duties of 'managing, maintaining and operating as agents of the Commission.

The Bill passed through Parliament with little change, the 2nd reading of the Bill took place on December 18th 1946 and was carried by 362 votes to 204 and after being given Royal Ascent in the August of the following year, the Transport Act, 1947 was written into the statute.

It is not intended here to provide a copy of the Act, nor to explain the 128 Sections and 15 Schedules which went to make up the piece of legislation. However, a few paragraphs outlining its effect on goods transport by road are provided.

In Part 1 of the Act, the first 11 sections dealt with the British Transport Commission, how it was to be set up, its powers, general duty, the Executives, Consultative Committees, acquisition by agreement and compulsory purchase of land.

In Part 3 there were 17 sections dealing with the acquisition of undertakings by the BTC, including those operating under A- and B-licences either wholly or partly, which operated on ordinary long-distance carriage for hire and reward.

An explanation is given as to what was meant by long distance -i.e. forty miles or upwards. Plus an explanation as to what would not be treated as ordinary long distance carriage.

The Notice of Acquisition had to be in writing to the person carrying on the undertaking, who also had to reply in writing if they contended that the Act did not apply to them. An arbitration tribunal would be set up to hear arguments where there was disagreement

Other sections dealt with contracts, mergers, date of transfer under acquisition, amount of compensation, method of paying compensation, and the duty of the operator to maintain their business from the date of Notice to the actual day of Acquisition.

Further sections dealt with the measure of compensation for cessation of business, meaning of 'operating centre', amendments to Road and Rail Traffic Act 1933, and reference to Defence Permits.

There were other numerous provisions dealing with finance, accounts and statistics, pensions, staff and expenses, and the establishment of Transport Arbitration Tribunal.

Soon after the Act important voluntary acquisitions took place, notably of H. & G. Dutfield and Transport Services, enabling the appointment of Henry T. Dutfield, of H. & G. Dutfield and Claude Barrington, Chairman of Transport Services to the RTE Board. (His replacement as Chairman of the RHA was B.G. Turner, Managing Director of Thomas Allen, who was to complain regularly about the difficulties of negotiating with the RTE/RHE.

The acquisition and transfer on 1st January 1948 of the Railways shareholdings in road transport companies (see table 1) enabled the resources of Hays Wharf, with Pickfords and, Carter Paterson with the other companies, to form the basis for managing the planned acquisition and integration of some 3,400 undertakings, (Pickfords turnover was 73% excluded

traffic). Thomas Tilling, regarded as a bus operator, was to contribute some 880 goods vehicles with 120 horses. Sir Frederick Heaton had already stated in Tillings 1946 Annual report, 'he was in favour of integration, and if nationalisation was the only way to it, so be it'.

There was a substantial, mainly London based, Contract Hire business including Pickfords, Tillings, and Chas. A. Wells, McNamara and N.M.U. depots. There were also undertakings at Manchester; Foulkes & Bailey and also N.M.U; and at Glasgow, Taylors. The RTE Divisions and Groups were however, slow in entering Contract Hire.

The RTE started with a nucleus of staff, not all familiar with road transport, but it was fortunate in being able to fill posts from the staff from these, and the early voluntary acquisitions.

The majority of former owners or managers who joined BRS on acquisition of their undertakings, appeared to be able to accept the changes necessary, and were to be involved in the successful integration, and the development of new services.

Above: The scene outside the House of Commons in 1947, when many of the free enterprise hauliers gathered, to hand in the Road Hauliers Petition to Parliament. The very clean Austin tilt van which carried copies of the Petition, was supplied by H.& G. Dutfield Ltd, for Mr. H. Dutfield was a very keen supporter of the campaign to keep road haulage free from State interference. In the event, the Petition had little effect on the outcome of the 1947 Act, H.& G. Dutfield became H. & G. Dutfield (BTC) Ltd when it was voluntarily acquired by the BTC, and in fact Mr. H. Dutfield himself became a part-time member of the Road Transport Executive.

Among these were the linking of the Districts and groups by a dedicated network of over 200 teleprinters at a cost of £180,000 plus £62.10s.0d per printer. The first 'Roll on, Roll-off' ferry service was also acquired at this time.

Of course some found they were unable to work within the constraints imposed and were to leave, or had their service

Table 1 - Road Freight Companies owned by the Railway Companies and transferred to the Road Haulage Executive

Hays Wharf Cartage Co. Ltd.
GWR, LM&SR, L&NER, and SR.
(each 25%).

Carter Paterson & Co. Ltd.
T. Ball & Co Ltd.
Beans Express Ltd.
Carter Paterson (Midland) Ltd.*
Carter Paterson (North Western) Ltd.*
Carter Paterson (Southern) Ltd.*
City & Suburban Carriers Ltd.*
England's & Perrott's Ltd.
Express Motor & Body Works Ltd.
Herd & Gerner Ltd.
Hernu, Heron & Stockwell Ltd.
Karriers Parcel Delivery Ltd.*
Leicester & County Carriers Ltd.*
Liverpool Parcel Delivery Co. Ltd.*
South Coast Carriers Ltd.

Southern Carriers Ltd.
Swift Parcel Delivery Service Ltd.*
Sutton & Co. Ltd. (50%).
Sutton & Co. (Manchester) Ltd (50%).
T. & D. Carriers Ltd.

Pickfords Ltd.
Arthur Batty Ltd.
Benefit Tyre Co. Ltd.
H. Bentley & Co. (Bradford) Ltd.
Chaplins Ltd.*
Coulson & Co. Ltd.
Couchers (I of W.) Ltd.
Express Transport Service
 (Wellingborough) Ltd.
Garlick, Burrell & Edwards Ltd.
A. J. Hewett & Co. Ltd.
Hughes Bros. Ltd.
Pickfords, France S.A. (Paris).

Shepherd Bros (I of W.) Ltd.
Venn & MCPherson Ltd.

Currie & Co. (Newcastle) Ltd.
L&NER (50%)

Joseph Nall & Co. Ltd. LM&SR

James Petrie. LM&SR

Wordie & Co Ltd. LM& SR (51%)
Herbert Davidson Ltd.
James Dickson Ltd.
Dumfries & Galloway Transport Ltd.
Road Engines & Kerr Ltd.
South Western Transport Ltd.
John Russell & Son Ltd.

*Indicates Carter Paterson & Pickfords Joint Parcels Service Associated Companies. (also Tersons, Building Contractors were at least part owned in 1947).

The following is a list of Acquired 'household' names that G.W. Quick Smith, Secretary/Legal Advisor to the R.T.E., considered should be listed for posterity.

A.V. Hill Ltd.
Bouts Tillotson Ltd.
Bristol Haulage Ltd.
Bulk Haulage Ltd.
C.A. & F. Cook. Ltd.
Carter Paterson Ltd.
Chesterfield Transport Ltd.
Currie & Co. (Newcastle) Ltd.

Davies & Brownlow Ltd.
Eastern Roadways Ltd.
Ex-Army Transport Ltd.*
Fisher Renwick Ltd.
John Grocock Ltd.
Hills Storage (Melton) Ltd.
Holdsworth & Burrill Ltd.
Holdsworth & Hanson Ltd.
Joseph Hanson Ltd
Manchester Storage & Transport Ltd.
McNamara & Co. Ltd.
Metropolitan Transport Supply Co Ltd.

Joseph Nall Ltd.
North Western Transport Services Ltd
O.K. Carrier Co. Ltd.
Ormsher & Timpson Ltd.
P. X. Ltd.
South Coast Carriers Ltd.
Southern Roadways Ltd.
Sutton & Co. (Manchester) Ltd.
Swindon Transport Ltd.
Taunton Transport Services Ltd.
Wallsend Road Haulage Ltd.
Warrington Transport Ltd.

*This became North Western Transport Services - Did Q.S. forget?

ended. George Read, Peterborough, retained as a consultant, wrote to his local paper with criticisms of BRS operations, and was given notice for this. W.H. Bowker was dismissed through a reluctance to place the lion crest on the vehicles under his control, being quoted as considering there was only one lion there.

Among successful appointments was that of A Parker, Senior Road Haulage Officer, RHA Eastern Region, appointed Norwich District Manager. This was followed by what became known as the East Anglia experiment, with the appointment of an Area Freight Superintendent for Norfolk, Suffolk and part of Essex. The intention here was to send the London bound freight traffic from Norwich and Ipswich by rail; that for all other destinations would go by road. It was not to become a permanent service.

Why Voluntary acquisitions? Once it was known that the Labour party manifesto would include the nationalisation of road transport, influential members of the industry, notably Sir Maxwell Hicks, Robert Hanson, Oliver Holdsworth, Major Gustav Renwick, and of course Claude Barrington, (who had long prophesied the nationalisation of the industry), suggested

that it would be in the best interests of this to obtain the agreement of owners of former units of the RHO to sell voluntarily and thereby create the nucleus of BRS. In return they would be paid directly in cash as an incentive. Hence the creation of the (BTC) Companies.

Also a factor to be considered was that many of these owners were approaching or at retirement age and now weary, austerity was still continuing and new vehicles were scarcer because of the need to export, fuel remained rationed, and labour - probably the biggest factor - was a problem, not least in quality.

Notifications of vacancies remained in force, drivers and other staff could only be recruited through Labour Exchanges, (Job Centres), or scheduled agencies. Firms could advertise their jobs, but applicants had to apply through the Exchange. There was constant concern over loss of equipment e.g. sheets, tyres, even batteries. Thefts from consignments of scarce or rationed items too were common, not helped by attempts to obtain clean signatures so that their firm would not suffer would only cause even more complaints. So it was reasonable for them to accept the inevitable, but also try to ensure that the new service would continue successfully.

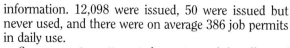

There was some irony in the appointment of Harold Elliot, General Manager of Pickfords, to be Chief Officer, Freight, RTE, then RHE. Pickfords had always excluded general haulage from its operations. A report of a talk by him in December 1948 noted he considered "of the executives BRS had much the more difficult task with hundreds of small businesses, rail having only four large companies. Much had to be done on the organisation of traffic, accounts, data and return loads. There was also the growth in C licences".

Quick Smith had been released from his post as secretary of the Road Haulage Association in February 1948, to become the secretary/legal advisor to the RTE. He had also been secretary of Road Transport Federation, until the division into the RHA, the Passenger Vehicle Operators Association (PVOA) and the Traders Road Transport Association (TRTA). He also had considerable experience of the war-time controls of road haulage.

He considered the Act as a legitimate means of depriving hauliers of their long distance business, giving them compensation. Therefore it was not iniquitous, even if it meant the haulier had to go to his competitor to obtain the permit to get his living. Because of this reasoning he was referred to as a 'Vicar of Bray'.

Both before and after his joining the RHE he was to write regularly in the technical press on appropriate subjects including the new Road Haulage Wages Council (the RHE had been required to agree to local wage scales and conditions). His articles became the authority for hauliers to understand the Act, especially those on negotiations for compensation on acquisition. He was at pains to explain Permits and their purpose of:

Allowing sub-contract work to be undertaken by the haulier which BRS was unable to do.
Allowing a period of time for the haulier before the acquisition process took effect.

Note: no permits would be granted if the applicant haulier was under notice of acquisition.

There were seven types of permit:

PR 1. ORIGINAL. This allowed the haulier to continue to operate for hire and reward from the base date of 28th November 1946, for up to three years after a first year interim period. These permits could be transferred i.e. sold. They were to have particular application for Furniture Removers.
PR 2. ORDINARY. To be applied for on a form supplied by the issuing Unit, usually for a period fixed by the Unit. There was very limited appeal if refused. It was not transferable. There were instances of BRS Units being accused of going after the work specified on the permit.
PR 3. A Substitute Permit.
PR 4. A Job Permit. Valid only for a specific job for the named customer.
PR 5. Ordinary Permit. Restricted to a specified vehicle.
PR 7. (also with PR4). Vehicle Pass, the driver having to show this on demand to any authorised person e.g. Vehicle Examiner.

By June 1949 over 17,250 applications for permits were reported, but many were unsupported by the necessary information. 12,098 were issued, 50 were issued but never used, and there were on average 386 job permits in daily use.

Some operators attempted to get round the effects of the 25-mile limit by applying to establish a new operating base away from the present base or bases. These were almost always refused, a notable exception being A. Pannell Ltd. who having been unable to use bases because of the War, were able to get these allowed as additions to their licence conditions.

Quick Smith was responsible for the successful introduction of the administration and legalities of acquiring and then operating the undertakings that were to comprise BRS. Such was the work load entailed that he successfully asked for the start of compulsory acquisitions and the associated 25 mile limit to be delayed, in the event compulsory acquisitions began January 1949.

The members of the Board of the RHE were:

Chairman:
Major General G.N. Russell. He was described as hard working, energetic in seeing for himself and good at setting the agenda for their meetings.

Full time Members:
Claude Barrington, a Chartered Engineer, formerly Managing Director of Transport Services, and responsible for its development into a public quoted company. He had a practical commercial attitude, always supporting the Chairman. (Later, from 1956, he was to be the successful Chairman of BRS Parcels).

George Cardwell, formerly Director of Thomas Tilling. He went to the Road Passenger Executive when this was formed in June 1949. Some of his responsibilities, particularly Engineering and Stores, were to be taken over by George Sinclair, Chief Planning and Supplies Officer, London Transport.

Harold Clay, formerly Assistant General Secretary, Transport & General Workers Union. He came to be regarded as a 'father figure', enjoying public speaking and played an important role in establishing training and development courses. He was also involved in creating the negotiating structure between BRS and the appropriate trade union organisations.

Archie Henderson, previously Chairman of the Traffic Commissioners, Scottish Licensing Authority and formerly of the T.& G.W. Union. Generally constructive, but he could be difficult if affronted. He held strong political views, frequently disagreeing with Barrington.

Part-time Members:
W. Beckett. A Trade Union nominee who, having no connection with transport, moved over to the RPE.

Henry T. Dutfield. Managing Director of H. & G. Dutfield. First Chairman of the re-organised RHA. 1945-46. Although he was criticised for taking up this appointment by many members of the RHA, their Express Carriers Functional Group sent him a letter of congratulation, dated 22th February 1948, on this appointment. Known to Quick Smith, when member of

Road Rail Advisory Committee. Known also to lose the agendas for the meetings. Well regarded, he was considered to have held his own in a hard world.

P.T.R. Tapp. Managing Director of Market Transport, (Smithfield Market meat hauliers), associated with Quick Smith in the formation of the Meat Transport Organisation. An associated business was County Commercial Cars, at that period specialist body builders, and Fordson six wheel chassis specialists.

On appointment as Chairman of the Board of the RHE, Major-General G.N. Russell announced his objective as:

"To organise the road transport services of the country so that they give the public, a flexible and efficient service which meets their needs and which is so integrated with other forms of transport that the best possible use is made of all forms of transport".

The Chairman's salary on appointment was £5,000 per annum, Full-time members received £3,500 per annum and Part-time members £1,500 By comparison a driver would be paid 2/6d per hour, (12½p) and a Hays Wharf skilled fitter's London hourly rate was 2/9d (about 14p).

BRS was required to operate within the concept that it was and should be a public service. The long distance general haulage monopoly - free from haulage licensing, (and road tax) -to integrate with rail. Traffics should be directed to the most appropriate mode, including waterways, but rail if possible. (However, the exemption of the own account C licence operator, allowing them to pick and chose their method of carrying their traffic meant that this grand plan was doomed, indeed by 1951 it was recognised as not going to be possible).

In planning the management and organisation, the Board had to ensure it was able to carry out three distinct tasks:

i). Acquisition and transfer of the undertaking to the RHE, then BRS, with agreement of all details of the transfer and of payment.
ii). To build up the organisation into which these undertakings could operate.
iii). Provide an uninterrupted road transport service to customers, and profitably.

It did not know how many undertakings would be acquired, as the 'long distance formula', had to be applied to every undertaking. On being served a 'Notice of Acquisition', the owner could object on the grounds he was not predominately long distance. If such an owner made no objection, the error made no difference. The RHE had to serve the Notice if it thought an undertaking came within their scope. The Permit system allowed a range of choices to the applicant, who could demand or not to be acquired wholly or in part.

The RHE Board had a collective responsibility for the management of BRS on behalf of the BTC. Each Director having special responsibilities, e.g. Barrington had responsibility for Mechanical and Civil Engineering, (at first shared with George Cardwell), and also for Freight Traffic, Operations, Commercial Rates and Claims. By any standard this was a considerable work load, not made easier by his Officer for Organisational Research and Charges, J.W.S. Nicholls, (ex McNamara) failing in health and leaving soon after. Nicholls would have been appointed a Director of the RTE but for the delay in the acquisition of McNamara.

McNamara, a Publicly quoted company, were to lose their Royal Mail contract in May 1947 but had an option of continuing with much of their town and country parcels and smalls section and the contract hire fleet, and selling off surplus premises. After a special meeting it was decided to use Section 42(i) of the Act to be acquired. This was agreed and McNamara joined BRS on 1st July 1948. Co-incidentally the other London Royal Mail contractor was H. & G. Dutfield.

Harold Clay was responsible for Establishment, Staff and Welfare. He and Quick Smith met with Sir Roubert Gould, Permanent Secretary, Minister of Labour. This led to the establishment of a tri-partite Joint Council; BRS, RHA and appropriate Employees organisations, i.e. trade unions. There was a place for arbitration if agreement was not reached. The only difficulty was that Frank Cousins, T.& G.W. Union, would not accept BRS acting as Secretary. The system of annual pay award, and J.I.C. local agreements was one result.

BRS had a variety of conditions and wage and salary structures. They had 4,000 women employees, from Unit managers to horse keepers. Harold Clay, Stanley Raymond, NUR, and Frank Cousin also established a co-operative relationship although with railway influences. The fair wage clause implied in the 1933 Act had never been applied by a Licensing Authority.

The two part-time members also had specific responsibilities. Dutfield was Chairman; Board of Management, Pickfords-Special Traffics Division, and Tapp was Chairman of the Vehicles Committee.

The RHE organisation was based on line and staff, initially three tier:- Headquarters; Chief Officer. Then came the eight Divisional Managers with their own Divisional Officers e.g. Divisional Engineer. (It was possible for a Divisional Officer, i.e. Divisional Engineer to seek to consult with his Chief Officer). Below this second tier, the Districts, each with a District Officer. See appendices for Divisions, Groups etc.

There were eight BRS Divisions, each with a distinctive divisional colour code:-

A. South Eastern.	(Royal Blue).	44 Groups.
B. Scottish.	(Traffic Blue).	27 Groups.
C. North Western.	(Sea Green).	31 Groups.
D. North Eastern.	(Road Haulage Red).	36 Groups.
E. Midland.	(Nut Brown).	36 Groups.
F. South Western.	(Road Haulage Green).	19 Groups.
G. Western.	(Lead Grey).	14 Groups.
H. Eastern.	(Turquoise Blue).	24 Groups.

Note: A Division's vehicle was identified by its colour, this surrounding the lion crest on the cab door.

The ninth Division, Pickfords, dealt with Special Traffics.

Special Traffics comprised of five of the excepted or excluded traffics: Bulk liquids, Explosives, Meat, Household Furniture - including for a period new furniture, and Abnormal/Indivisible Loads. It would follow that any relevant operations of acquired undertakings were transferred to Pickfords. In Leeds for example this led to the removals operations of Holdsworth & Hanson, J. Bragg, Butterwick & Walker, A. Hopkinson and A. Hudson, all placed under the control of Pickfords Removals Leeds office.

E. Bulgin, Manager of Pickfords' Wood Lane, Birmingham Branch told a meeting of the Institute of Transport of some of the problems of heavy haulage, not least being the extra mileage because of bridge and road restrictions, (This being

ROAD TRANSPORT EXECUTIVE

DIVISIONAL MAP

SCOTTISH DIVISION
DIVISIONAL MANAGER —
J. B. HASTIE,
150, HOPE STREET,
GLASGOW
Telephone GLASGOW DOUGLAS 7446

NORTH-EASTERN DIVISION
DIVISIONAL MANAGER :—
N. C. McPHERSON,
53, CLARENDON ROAD,
LEEDS, 2.
Telephone : LEEDS 30845

MIDLAND DIVISION
DIVISIONAL MANAGER —
SIR H. REGINALD KERR,
5, NORFOLK ROAD,
EDGBASTON,
BIRMINGHAM, 15.
Telephone : BIRMINGHAM EDGBASTON 1186

NORTH-WESTERN DIVISION
DIVISIONAL MANAGER :—
W. E. C. MACVE,
c/o FISHER RENWICK, LTD.,
WHITE CITY,
CHESTER ROAD,
MANCHESTER, 16.
Telephone : TRAFFORD PARK 1869

EASTERN DIVISION
DIVISIONAL MANAGER :
J. B. GARRETT,,
9, QUEEN STREET,
NORWICH.
Telephone : NORWICH 25192

WESTERN DIVISION
DIVISIONAL MANAGER :—
J. FREEGUARD,
4/5, MOUNT STUART SQUARE,
CARDIFF.
Telephone : CARDIFF 4776/7

SOUTH-WESTERN DIVISION
DIVISIONAL MANAGER —
A. J. WRIGHT,
c/o SOUTHERN ROADWAYS
(1936) LTD.,
WEST SHORE WHARF,
POOLE, DORSET
Telephone : POOLE 245

SOUTH-EASTERN DIVISION
DIVISIONAL MANAGER :
F. C. G. MILLS,
c/o TRANSPORT SERVICES
(B.T.C.), LTD.,
116, OLD BROAD STREET,
LONDON, E.C.2.
Telephone : LONDON WALL 5586

October, 1948.

SCALE OF MILES
0   10   20   30   40   50   60   70   80

before the advent of the motorways). Rugeley to Leeds was a 180-mile journey, rather than normal 110 miles. Birmingham to Hull took 262 miles instead of 158 miles.

He also told of the problems of integrating acquisitions, mostly the men, who after years of regarding Pickfords as competitors, found it difficult to change. This led to constant claims of bias for overtime, and for the choice work. He informed the meeting that fifteen years after the Norman E. Box men joined Wood Lane, there would still be protests about perceived (and unjustified) unfairness.

Other problems he outlined included heated discussions at the changes of solid tyres. It was always possible, but unpredictable, that a new solid tyre would separate from its rim after a very small mileage, causing problems, delay and replacement on the road, usually at an inconvenient point. The old, if worn tyre could be relied upon, and there was a tendency to try to keep them as long as possible. This did not always meet with the Engineers Department's agreement.

The eight Divisions were subsidiaries, and were to have between 2,000 and 8,000 vehicles; there was further sub-division into the 30 Districts, each having between 1,000 and 2,000 vehicles. The Districts which were sub-subsidiaries were further divided into Groups, in all some 200, with between 100 to 300 vehicles. Finally there were the Units or Depots, 1,000 in all with between five and 250 vehicles.

The RTE/BRS vehicle colours and livery was a very early decision and these were as follows:

General (flat/sided) vehicles: Red, red wheels and
　　　　　　　　　　　　　　　　white lettering.
Parcels and Smalls vehicles: Green, red wheels and
　　　　　　　　　　　　　　　　white lettering.
Special Traffics: Blue, red wheels and white lettering.

The night trunk vehicles had illuminated headboards, one of the first introductions to become readily noticed. Luton vans had the glass panel inserted in the front panel. The practice became a point of protest from Fire Chiefs, who considered this caused confusion with fire and emergency vehicles. It was discontinued in 1953.

The tipping group fleets, or units with tipping traffic had their tipping vehicles in grey. Almost all the acquired general tipping work, other than contract work was discontinued by BRS after 1953, not least because of problems with rates, in Quick Smith's view because of the 'doubtful legality' within that area of the transport industry.

Negotiations for voluntary acquisitions ended in July 1948 and by the end of the year 248 of those agreed, with some 8,200 vehicles and 1867 horses, had been absorbed. The turnover for this first year of operations was £13.5 million.

Very early on parcels was segregated from general traffic, and placed under the control of N.D. Fawkner, the Deputy Chief Officer, previously with Carter Paterson. Where 'smalls' had been only part of the acquired undertakings business, or it was a small business this was integrated into Carter Paterson, or the most appropriate Parcels unit. The former largest independent parcels and smalls undertakings, the Holdsworth and Hanson/Bouts Tillotson companies, Fisher Renwick (English bases) and PX, were to continue as virtually separate Parcels units until the formation of BRS Parcels in 1953 as part of the changes brought about by the 1953 Transport Act.

The re-organisation of the South Eastern division into functional groups led to a new parcels district being created.

The City Area: Comprised the former Carter Paterson & Pickfords Joint Service with Sutton, and a few London bases of small carriers. It carried only parcels traffic, together with a shipping service.

The Metropolitan Area: Initially comprised virtually the London bases of all the independent Parcels and Smalls carriers. This led to a staged integration, and occasionally separation, of the parcels and smalls part of the business, eg Fisher Renwick Muswell Hill group was transferred to Parcels district from 24th. March 1951, as was the Borough group, the former Dawsons and Routh & Stevens businesses. The Metropolitan Area had more Smalls than Parcels traffic and therefore had a greater number of flats than the City area.

Note: By February 1953 all depots and vehicles were coded in the 33A series in the Gazetteer/Directory.

Quick Smith was understandably proud of the efficient routine that enabled the speedy transfer of undertakings to take place once the details had been agreed. Particularly noteworthy was the transfer of the 52 Transport Arrangement member companies with 1,300 vehicles (see appendices, page 148). This had been revived at the end of the RHO, having retained its pre-war basis of membership by invitation only.

The legal transfer took place at the same time for each of the companies, without hitch. This was carried out by forming a special company, T.A. Realisations. On the Thursday before the Friday chosen for the transfer, each company was told the transfer was to take place. The mass meeting of 52 groups of appropriate directors was held to agree general approval, this being followed by their resignations. A new board for the new (BTC) Companies, with the new British Transport Commission Directors immediately transacted the legal formalities to establish BRS as the new owners.

All the (BTC) voluntary acquisitions were to carry out their transfer in the same way, and all were to hold quarterly meetings, soon to be transferred to 222 Marylebone Road, until about November 1959.

The predetermined programme for the despatch of mandatory notices for compulsory acquisition started in October 1948 for vesting to be effective from 7th January 1949. Some 2,000 notices - of a possible 3,000 plus - had been issued by October 1951, when the newly elected Conservative Government stopped new acquisitions taking place.

Legal services could have been a problem, but fortunately Clifford, Turner & Co., a major City of London legal firm, for some reason had a team of solicitors surplus to their immediate needs at this time. They undertook to co-ordinate the Executives legal work in acquiring undertakings for the remarkably low charge of £50 for each transferred undertaking.

C. Johnson, previously Secretary, Transport Services, was the Officer for the Acquisitions section at Headquarters. No doubt their own record of acquiring some 60 businesses since the formation in 1936 was helpful.

A problem with private companies was non-availability of their trading details. The notice for acquisition had to be served if the RHE considered the undertaking came within the definition in the Act. The owner could object. Under Section 51 of the Act, the Licensing Authorities could provide details if requested.

Firms considered for compulsory acquisition were required to give the following information:

i). Their legal or registered name, registered address and the usual place of business.
ii). The number of vehicles owned, type of licences or permits, type of operation; General haulage, etc.
iii). The area covered, only normal journeys or work.
iv). If they were controlled under the RHO; hired as an operator, or if vehicle(s) were hired.
v). Associated concerns, or subsidiaries, offices or depots in other traffic areas.

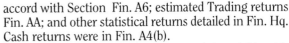

The acquisition compensation was based on:

Vehicles: current replacement value, less one fifth per year for age. There was also an allowance for betterment, or a deduction for worsenment, being based on the actual condition for the age.
Properties: a problem - some were not to be transferred, or the business operated without any.
Goodwill: (two-five years annual profits).
Overheads (or severance).

A considerable number of premises were excluded by agreement, as also were a large number of tenancies. These exclusions which were often arrived at after much negotiation, represented a very considerable financial capital saving to the Commission.

The vehicle current replacement value clause was to cause endless dispute being agreed sometime after the transfer. The acquired fleets comprised every make, type, age, condition and idiosyncrasy of the owners. For instance, Beckett Brothers, Fenton, Stoke-on-Trent, had the last working fleet of Armstrong Saurer Samson rigid eight wheeled lorries, with their own private 'scrap dump' providing spares. Blythe and Berwick, Leeds, also had a venerable fleet. Their agreed £40,000 compensation was only settled after arbitration. (Philip Blythe was also Chairman, Leeds, Goole and Hull Transport, Canal Carriers, and was to have to deal with both the RHE and the Docks & Inland Waterways Executive).

A schedule was compiled to be used as the basis for negotiations on the period of the working life. There were some disagreements over value with vehicles that had been modified, and kept in use for a longer period. This included some of the largest undertakings.

The transfer procedure was now routine. The directors or owners meeting approving the transfer. Safe custody of the documents was agreed, including copies of the AQ3 forms which provided details and valuation of all transferred assets, the vehicles, plant, equipment, premises. These were signed off by the Secretary or Accountant to form the basis for paying compensation. (For a period valuers did well from their commissions in negotiating the compensation to be paid).

An introduction to the RHE Management Manual, and the procedures took place, with the required returns being explained. The management manual was the key to the Headquarters control of the Units. It had loose-leaf sections for each of the ten Headquarters departments. It was placed in use section by section.

That dealing with financial statistics, based on four-week periods was vital. The returns required covered; estimated trading, vehicle usage, working operating days, vehicles standing by, under repair or not available. ('Standing by' caused misunderstandings - a vehicle loaded on Friday night or Saturday morning for a Monday start was to be returned as working, not standing by). Financial statistics had to be in

accord with Section Fin. A6; estimated Trading returns Fin. AA; and other statistical returns detailed in Fin. Hq. Cash returns were in Fin. A4(b).

New bank accounts had to be opened, invariably with the same bank. A notable difference was an automatic channelling of receivables into a separate interest paid current account.

Headquarters and Division also required:

a). Particulars of all the staff on the date of transfer, their date of engagement, their present post, duties, full or part time, salary or wage, the date and amount of the last increase.
b). Terms of any service agreements, with details of any bonus or commission schemes, based on the preceding financial years profits.
c). Details of any pensions or life insurance schemes, (more common than might be thought, particularly with the parcels and smalls carriers).
d). Details of any outside commercial or professional interests of anyone involved in the under-taking.
e). The cars owned by the undertaking, and users, or cars privately owned, used for undertakings business.
f). The details of all current insurances, to include all policies, the issuing companies policy number, type i.e. fire, goods in transit, cover and renewal date; the premium rate, any discount. The agent and any commission receivable.

Some 15,000 separate policies were to be taken over; from 1st January 1951 all policies in force were cancelled, replaced by a new BRS Policy. Under the agreement the premium averaged £54 per vehicle per year, this was achieved by sharing the risk. When after claims were settled, one third of any surplus was received by BRS, if there was a deficiency BRS would pay two-thirds to the insurers.

Apart from parcels and smalls undertakings, the administration of most of the acquisitions could fairly be described as simple. The new standardised operating procedures introduced for general haulage operations were not difficult to use, and were designed to give customers a quick response to their enquiries, and also avoiding wasteful empty running.

When an order or enquiry was received, either by phone or letter, it was entered into the order book (Ops1) and allocated a consecutively running job number. When a vehicle was allocated, or became available, the details of the job were transferred to the job consignment note (Ops4), The single entry note system was used. This was in four parts, the top three pages, yellow, pink and blue, were given to the driver, the fourth copy was filed.

If the traffic was a distance or trunk consignment, and sub-contracted to another group's vehicle or a one belonging to an undertaking not yet acquired, a sub contractors confirmation note (Ops5) was made out, the top copy to be posted to the that vehicle's own depot. When the traffic was carried on of the group's own vehicles, a vehicle advice note (Ops7) was made out, and despatched to the depot to which the vehicle is to report to when the consignment has been delivered.

At the end of each day, daily traffic summaries were made out from form Ops1. The first Summary (Ops2) showed traffic carried on the group's own vehicles. Traffic tonnages received from other Groups, were to be entered under the sub heading 'Traffic carried on own vehicles, but received from other BRS groups'. The second summary (Ops3) showed the sub-contracted traffic carried by non BRS vehicles. The arrival and despatch of 'foreign' vehicles was recorded on a separate form (Ops8).

The new Manager of a Unit had instructions to deal with all official correspondence, and in particular to submit at his next Board meeting, and all subsequent ones, a brief report on all matters, finance, operations, engineers, stores and property. Capital expenditure not exceeding £100 could be approved by the Manager, subject to approval at the next Board meeting. It was not to be exceeded. Expenditure over £100 could not be incurred without approval of the Board; any over £200 needed previous confirmation by the Division or Divisional Manager. The same guidelines applied to disposal of assets, other than vehicles.

Disposals of vehicles were dealt with by the Engineer, after first being offered to other units. At this period it was the policy that all vehicles sold out of service must be dismantled for scrap or spares, and buyers had to give a guarantee to this effect. Their registration log books were retained.

Communication between Headquarters and the operating units was effective, Each Division, (subsidiary) and its Districts (sub-subsidiaries), had a meeting every two months attended by the Board of the District who were the Divisional Manager, the Divisional Accountant and the District Manager. The minutes of these meetings, together with the relevant four weekly financial reports being assessed by Headquarters.

Every two months there was also a Headquarters conference, reviewing a Division, with the Divisional Officers and their District Managers.

There was also a Chief Officers Committee, Quick Smith acting as Chairman, to serve as a link between the Board and their Chief Officers. It dealt with matters remitted to it by the Board, and co-ordinating actions affecting more than one of the ten departments. The committee was also able to make proposals for consideration by the Board.

The Engineers had a difficult time, having to deal with ever increasing numbers of vehicles, assessing them and allocating them to groups or units to achieve as standard a fleet as possible in make, type, and capacity. The needs of traffic or customers could mean a non standard chassis remaining at a unit, simply because of its special body. Coventry 2E had a concentration of JNSN (Jensen) flats, because of their ability to carry the grey Ferguson tractor currently being manufactured at that company's Banner Lane works.

Another problem for the interchangeability of vehicles - especially with Parcels Group depots - was the use of either the Scammell automatic coupling or the fifth wheel (SAE) type turntable.

Deliveries of new vehicles were on an extended delivery date, at the end of 1949 BRS had taken over the orders, placed by undertakings before their acquisition, for 4,100 new vehicles. Every order was taken-over, with some substitutes for more suitable types of chassis being arranged.

To improve the fleet standard, many of vehicles regarded as being in unacceptable condition were re-conditioned. This was planned with some care as to cost effectiveness. Consideration also had to be given to the trades own difficulties, including availability of spares and skilled labour. Use was made of:

Manufacturer's service at their works or depots.
Dealers depots or workshops.
Suitable acquired ancillary facilities.

Some use was made of London Transport's Chiswick and Charlton works to re-condition AEC engines. It was later reported that BRS workshops were able to do this at a lower cost.

Engineering facilities and practices at the acquired undertakings varied from D.I.Y., employing one or two mechanics, using the local dealer or an outside workshop for all but routine services, to the generally excellent workshops of the larger undertakings. An example of the latter was the Holdsworth & Hanson group which had also owned Oswald Tillotson, and retained an effective relationship with them. Another example was Transport Services' Star Bodies it being able to build 400 bodies a year and repairing about the same.

The RHE like the RPE was not allowed to manufacture for outside customers, nor build more than 25% of its bodies. Neither could it trade in vehicle spares or petrol. There was a three-year period of grace to sell these acquired facilities on. There were notable exceptions for petrol sales, particularly in Scotland. Stores received particular attention, being separated from engineering, with recording introduced to show use and costs. Some £2 million worth of unwanted obsolete stores 'items' were said to have been forced upon BRS. This included loss by theft after valuation.

Bulk use items, fuel, lubricants, tyres were the subject of national contracts. Tyres from a single manufacturer were specified for a group, with a back-up of national coverage for fitting and stocking. The tyre bill in 1952 was no less than £3.9 million! However, there was a downside to these national contracts as some small country and town garages undeniably suffered from their loss of this business.

Tables of operating lives for various makes and types of vehicles were compiled from the start, leading to a reduction in the depreciation period or the vehicles expected working life. That for a premium chassis being reduced from 12 years to eight. (See table 2).

Standard service programmes were introduced:

1). Daily driver check.
2). Inspection at four to six weeks.
3). Annual service.
4). Complete overhaul, refurbished to as new condition at four to five years service.

The policy for Workshops was:

Group Workshops - located at the major depots.
District Workshops - serving all groups in the District.
Divisional Workshops - serving all districts in a Division.
National Workshops - specialising in the overhaul of engines or major components.

At this period (1949/1951) the maintenance cost was quoted as averaging 3d (1.4p) per mile. The Engineers department was also responsible for introducing two separately wired rear lights, red reflectors each side and a white rear area for all 40,000 BRS vehicles.

By 1951 only four makes of maximum load (rigid eight wheeler) chassis were being ordered, they being standardised on wheel and tyre size, electrics, and air braking. Vacuum braking was now only accepted for outstanding orders.

With orders for 5,070 new vehicles outstanding, approval was given for the Bristol rigid eight wheeled chassis to be designed and built for BRS alone. First placed in service with 2F East Bristol Group late in 1952, it was followed by an equally successful maximum capacity articulated lorry in 1955. Both the unit and trailer were designed and built at Brislington.

Production of the rigid eight chassis was to cease in 1957 whilst the last HA tractor unit and last ST semi-trailer was to leave the Brislington works in 1964.

Property management was also an early problem, with compulsorily acquired properties being taken over at a rate sometimes exceeding ten per day. Even in late 1951 three per week could be dealt with. Some 800 properties were acquired with the ex railway and voluntary undertakings, most were able to absorb those small undertakings which previously operated from the owner's house or where the depot was no longer available. More suitable locations for some depots or extensions to others became an ongoing need.

Only Hays Wharf had had a property management department with technical staff. The newly appointed Chief Architect and his staff also had to deal with repairs, replacement proposals and the disposal of those acquired premises considered inadequate or redundant. Many of those acquired had limited parking, and almost none of the general haulage depots could deal with 100 vehicle fleets. A problem to be made worse by the Police, now becoming unhelpful with on-street parking. One notable example affected 27E Dudley Group, Brierley Hill unit prosecuted in May 1951 for seven vehicles parked outside the Kingswinford premises. It was submitted in defence that there was only room for four vehicles inside, although the allocation was fifty vehicles. A new depot was being built at Wordsley.

Another problem area was the City of Bristol where much adverse criticism was voiced due to the congestion in and

around the premises taken over - this led to fewer, but larger depots being allocated under the Bristol Development Plan with new workshops and depot facilities being constructed on the Bedminster Trading Estate.

New BRS depots were rarely rail-served, even if they were ex British Railways. Rail co-ordination was minimal, and usually for parcels trunking. Carter Paterson had had rail-linked depots at Croydon, Brighton and Bournemouth.

The 'A' South Eastern Division was immediately recognised as a problem. This was the centre for services to and from most of the country, with a tremendous diversity of traffic within a closely concentrated geographic area. Many of the larger acquired undertakings had their own depots or interworking arrangements which had to be considered, as their customers preferences would be affected with any changes or merging of units. Territorial groupings as originally set up had clearly defined boundaries - however changes were to be made as the emphasis now switched from directional to functional.

In 1951 the division was reduced in area, and merged into six groups, with 50 depots. The fleet would comprise 1,250 vehicles: 600 to be maximum gross vehicle weight; 400 10-ton articulated units; 250 local collection and delivery vehicles.

This replaced the earlier organisation with 7,816 vehicles, 1,300 on directional trunk traffic, 1,600 general haulage, 1,546 Home Counties. These were mostly transferred to F South Western Division. As an example of the savings possible, Islington 43A, with eight depots, 22 makes and 100 types, would be three units with only five makes and 25 types.

BRS was now able to benefit by operating from surplus former British Railways premises. Integration and co-ordination was no longer evident in BRS forward planning, There was no difficulty over problems with any driver surplus, these were dealt with by wastage, at that period a serious problem.

For the most part General Haulage trunk routes were continued, being extended and improved with nightly services, The unit responsible for terminal work at each end retained the revenue, introduced for efficient accounting. An unforeseen benefit from this was that BRS was allowed to retain many of its properties at the conclusion of the privatisation disposals.

Contracts were now a separate and increasingly important section, with some 1,600 vehicles, and making progress in attracting new customers, including some who had previously discontinued using BRS Contracts.

London Parcels section comprised some 1,500 vehicles out of the nation-wide total of 4,000 vehicles.

Scotland, B Division, too had been a problem, although different, in that no acquired undertaking had covered all Scotland, let alone the whole of England. By 1951 it was a unified operating division based on the four Scottish administrative areas - Aberdeen, Dundee, Edinburgh, and Glasgow, with 24 Groups having 180 depots and 3,500 vehicles, and 130 horses (at Aberdeen).

The former Charles Alexander unit 2B Old Ford Road, continued to handle the trunk fish traffic. Abingdon continued to be largely livestock traffic, and also continued to retail a considerable gallonage of petrol. Milk collection and delivery was proportionately very important traffic.

At first Scottish Parcels traffic was dealt with by the undertakings which had previously included this service, notably the Charles Alexander and Wm. Wisely, country carrier (outside boundary) rounds. Changes were made at Glasgow,

---

Table 2 - Replacement Vehicle Schedule

A. Tipping vehicles; any make or capacity - three years.

B. Private cars - five years.

C. Light vans - five years.

Vehicles over ten cwts to six tons capacity, including articulated Scammell units (i.e. mechanical horses).

D. Five years depreciation:

Austin	Bedford	Commer
Dodge	Ford	Jowett
Morris-Commercial	Reo.	

E. Eight years depreciation:

Albion	Dennis	ERF
Foden	Guy	International
JNSN	Karrier	Leyland
Maudslay	Pagefield	Scammell
Seddon	Thornycroft	Tilling Stevens
Vulcan		

Skips, Flats, Lift Vans (all capacities) - eight years.

Vehicles over six tons capacity, including articulated vehicles.

F. Ten years depreciation:

AEC	Albion	Atkinson
Crossley	Dennis	ERF
Foden	International	Karrier
Latil	Leyland	Maudslay
Scammell	Thornycroft	Unipower

Battery Electric vehicles: 12 years.
Drawbar trailers - four wheels: 15 years.

where Youngs Express Deliveries, Holdsworth & Hanson and Fisher Renwick were merged to form a Parcels Group, and a rare example of integration was the introduction of a Glasgow-London over-night parcels trunk using containers. It was claimed this saved about a third of the journey time between the terminal depots.

The rail cartage agencies held by Mutter Howey, Wordie and Cowan were continued mostly as general units. For historic reasons Scotland had an unusually high proportion of the railways cartage carried out by these agents. Some of this traffic was retained by B Division until the creation of National Carriers, although their individual identities were to disappear.

Not surprisingly because of the remote areas served, some 100 private haulage firms with about 1,000 vehicles remained, all but 80 being given three-year permits. An eye was kept upon their conduct, for example, a Campbeltown haulier with permit was prosecuted for excess hours and not keeping records when taking a load of herrings to Glasgow, this was as a result of a complaint by the Argyll Group Manager. BRS too had their own prosecutions over hours. At 63C White City Parcels depot, 61 drivers were summonsed for excessive hours - not for driving - but for working on the loading bank, after finishing their driving day.

De-nationalisation

Following the return of the Conservative Government in October 1951, the new Minister of Transport, A.T. (Alexander) Boyd, issued a White paper Cmnd 8538 with details of the proposed de-nationalisation. BRS was to be divided into Units and sold by tender. Existing permits would continue, as would the 25-mile radius limit, but there would be a greater latitude in granting or renewing licences. There would also be a levy on all operators, including own account C licencees, estimated to raise £4 million, based on £2 per ton unladen weight. This would be given to BRS to assist their costs over the transition period. Proving nothing is new; the question of how a 'leak' of the contents of the White Paper appeared first in MOTOR TRANSPORT was raised in Parliament.

To prepare for the anticipated reduction in size, early in 1952 BRS cut back the management layer at Group level, the chain now becoming Divisions, Districts, Units. District Managers became responsible for all operational and financial matters concerning their Districts, This meant the Managers of Units would no longer be expected to deal with technical problems, rather they would now concentrate on serving their customers. BRS also put up their general haulage rates by 7% from 24th February 1952, the RHA giving great publicity to the fact their members were not increasing their rates. This was unrealistic, and was not too helpful to them.

In the same year on an operational front, severe winter weather suffered in the North of England affected the A6 and Shap, and to help keep vehicles moving, two mobile supervisors with the use of two Land-Rovers assisted the County Council to try and keep the road open. They could employ labour, and had the use of two recovery vehicles based at Morecombe and Carleton.

In January 1953, the RHE was instructed to cut back and re-organise to prepare for the effects of de-nationalisation. This meant that Managers and staff from all departments would become redundant. Two effects of the RHE plans were the setting up of a separate Meat Haulage unit and the separation of the Parcels group, the intention being to offer them for tender as separate complete undertakings.

The first denationalisation Bill was to be delayed by the death of King George VI. The Transport Act 1953, was finally given the Royal Assent in November 1953. It was intended that BRS would now comprise no more than 2,341 vehicles with a total unladen weight of 13,906 tons. These would be on normal A licences, (restricting them to being based at one depot only), and BRS was now required to pay for Road Fund licences. The spares stock was reported as being valued at £4.75 million.

A Road Haulage Disposal Board was created, with Sir Malcolm Tristam Eve as Chairman. A member representing the interests of the private haulier was also appointed; R.H. Farmer, Managing Director of Atlas Express. De-nationalisation tenders were invited for some 700 Depots, Units etc., with some 5,000 vehicle only disposals. In total 125,000 lists and 700,000 catalogues were distributed.

Together, with the tender forms, no less than 4.4 million items were printed. Unsold or undervalued bids were re-offered and 20,000 vehicles were intended to be returned to the private sector. However, the programme ended with BRS retaining over 13,000 vehicles, and the Parcels - which actually commenced trading under the BRS (Parcels) Ltd name on 1st January 1955 - plus the Meat and Contracts units.

The RHE ceased to exist on 1st October 1953, being replaced by BRS. Major General G.N. Russell being appointed as Chairman of the new undertaking.

The full time members appointed were Claude Barrington, George Sinclair and G.W. Quick Smith. The part-time members were Harold Clay and George Henderson.

Generally negotiations, dealing with the disposals (of some 20,000 vehicles) and the future structure of the RHE and BRS leading to the 1956 Act, were to be conducted by Quick Smith.

Quick Smith summarised the pioneering years as follows:
The first task was to decide organisation, with a new national approach. It was departmentalised, with each manager at each level having complete responsibility for all functions within his sphere.

The pioneering years he described as thus:
1948: the year of planning.
1949: voluntary acquisitions.
1950: compulsory acquisitions.
1951: expansion.
1952: consolidation.

Other notable achievements he noted were:
There was now one insurance scheme, with third party liability for vehicles, and liability for goods in transit, with standard conditions of carriage. Engineering was now on a systematic basis.
There was a systematic and mechanical accounting system, and the previous conglomeration of rates varying from sub-standard to economic was now profitable.
There was obviously a great sense of enthusiasm by almost all staff from top to bottom, using resources only BRS could provide, also there was the opportunity to see what even small Units could or could not do.

Quick Smith however, also indicated there were the first signs that general haulage was to be a declining business.

Leading Acquisitions

A brief resume of three of the major road transport undertakings absorbed into the national fleet.

TRANSPORT SERVICES

The title Transport Services Ltd. (TS) was unknown to many people in the industry, because unlike some of the other large transport groups, vehicles carried the names of individual operating companies, and not that of the parent holding company.

There was however, one small form of group identity, and that was the way in which the fleet numbers were contained within a star emblem, usually on the front scuttle or wings. This identifying emblem led many drivers and others to acknowledge that the vehicles were 'part of the Star Group'. This was a plausible explanation when one remembers that the bodyshops of Transport Services located at Salford, was in fact Star Bodies Ltd.

The group holding company as Transport Services Ltd, was inaugurated with the formation of a public limited liability company, registered on 25th April 1936, with a capital of £130,000. Because of rapid progress within the group, the authorised capital was increased to £1 million in 1938.

Unlike some of its contemporaries. Transport Services Ltd was set up to bring together the activities of a number of individual haulage companies around the country. Whilst seeking to achieve economies of scale, no demands were made to diminish the identity nor independence of its constituent companies, so long as other companies within the group were given preference with regard to traffic and general assistance. Hence, Transport Services acted more as a guiding hand to its member companies, by helping with financial expertise, traffic generation, reduction of empty running, and other economies made possible by reason of its size and influence in the marketplace.

Because individual companies within the group catered for varying traffics and markets, there was no attempt at placing restrictions upon them, or to force any state of unwarranted amalgamations, or curtailment of individual approach in day-to-day operations.

A brief account of the many haulage companies that comprised the Transport Services group follows.

It is generally accepted that the major part of the British haulage industry came about following the end of the Great War, at a time when cheap motor lorries were available to satisfy the demands of the surge of ex servicemen, returning to 'civvy street' following the Armistice.

In Liverpool, a small group of individuals set up the Ex-Army Transportation Company, with the idea of providing work for some of the many new men who had bought their first lorry. By helping ex-comrades get started in business, the new company aimed to find loads for the budding new hauliers, as well as providing financial guidance and assistance to those in need.

The system flourished and expanded, first into Manchester and later into Glasgow, Leeds, Birmingham, Bristol and London. By 1928 it was necessary to put the organisation onto a more secure footing, and in May of that year a private limited company was registered as Ex-Army Transport Ltd, with an authorised capital of £10,000. The directors were listed as Samuel Royle, H.H. Houghton and C.S. Christensen, with Registered Offices at 5 Queen Street, Manchester.

By 1934 a fleet of 59 vehicles was listed, rising to 80 in 1936 and the round 100 being reached by 1939. At this time they were advertising services between Manchester, London, Liverpool, Birmingham, Hanley, Leeds, Bradford, Bristol, Hull, Glasgow, Dundee, Newcastle-on-Tyne and Nottingham.

Ex-Army Transport, or E.A.T. as it became known, was one of the founding members of Transport Services Ltd in 1936, and Samuel Royle became one of the directors of the new group company. Many years later in 1942, a change of title was arranged when the Ex-Army Transport Ltd was reconstituted as North Western Transport Services Ltd, a name which better indicated the area and scope of the haulage operation.

Under the embracing banner of Transport Services Ltd, North Western Transport Services Ltd (NWTS) passed to the control of the RHE early in the scheme of things, being listed as Ref:A15 under the Manchester heading with the address of 12 East Ordsall Lane, Salford. Other locations listed were: Butlin Street, Birmingham; Olympia Bldgs, Thornton Road, Bradford; Albert Road, St Phillips, Bristol; 36 West Street, Gateshead; 30 West Green Road, Stobcross, Glasgow; Waterloo Road, Hanley; 53 Walton Street, Hull; Marshall Street, Leeds; 14 Blackstock Street, Liverpool; Halling Wharf, Channelsea Road, Stratford, E15; and Triumph Road, Lenton, Notts.

Another early member of Transport Services was Donaldson Wright Ltd of Nottingham, which had its origins in 1919 when the Nottingham Chamber of Commerce set up a transport clearing house in order to assist its members with their transport problems. After a few years it was decided that the scheme was better served by being run on a more commercial basis, and so Mr Donaldson Wright, who had been managing the scheme, decided to continue the operations by setting up a private business.

Based broadly on services between the Nottingham area and London, the traffic was mainly of a 'smalls' nature, and gradually expanded in volume. A major expansion took place in 1937 when Holton's Transport Services of Long Eaton was acquired. In 1940, new and expanded premises were opened at Lenton, one of the Nottingham suburbs. Upon nationalisation the company was given the reference A23, with Triumph Road, Lenton and 5, Pentonville Road, London, N.1 being listed as premises. It later became Unit E6.

One of the most well-known fleets among Transport Services was undoubtedly that of General Roadways, whose fleet of Scammells epitomised long distance haulage in pre-nationalisation days. The origins of General Roadways goes back to the formation of Daniels Road Haulage, which was registered as a private company on 13th June 1930, with a capital of £100. The registered office was at 143 Anson Road, Cricklewood, and it is believed that two Scammells made up the original rolling stock.

The title of General Roadways Ltd dates from 17th March 1931 when the private company was registered with a capital of £100 and an office address listed as 145 Kingsland Road, E2. This new company, under the directorship of Claude Barrington and L.L. Godfrey, took over the Daniels Road Haulage business. By 1934 General Roadways Ltd (GR) was operating about 10 vehicles on an 'A' licence granted by the new Metropolitan Area of the Goods Vehicle Licensing system created by the Road & Rail Traffic Act, 1933.

Prior to the outbreak of World War II, G.R. had moved from Kingsland Road to premises at Spring Place, Kentish Town, NW5 and records show a fleet of 18 Scammell articulated vehicles operating under their A-licence.

In 1941 the business of C. Durston Ltd of Hailing Wharf, Channelsea Road, Stratford, E.15 was acquired by G.R., although it was already associated with T.S. by way of Donaldson Wright. Original details are not known, but by 1934 C. Durston, the proprietor, was listed as operating 14 vehicles on A-licence. Upon acquisition by T.S. it was incorporated as a private limited company with effect from 1st March 1938 with a capital of £10,000 and the fleet listed as 11 AEC, 7 Leyland, 2 Dennis and a Thornycroft. Added to the fleet of G.R. this produced a total fleet of some 40 vehicles.

In 1944 the T.S. group acquired the clearing house business carried on by Carey, Davis & Thomas Ltd which had branches in a number of large towns, and this was added to the G.R. business. Of possibly greater importance was the acquisition of a subsidiary company which had been set up in 1934 for the express purpose of supplying vehicles on contract hire. This contract hire company was titled C.D.& T. (Contracts) Ltd, and a new purpose-built garage had been built at Power Road, Chiswick in order to maintain the vehicles operated on a new contract negotiated with brewers Whitbread & Co. Ltd.

This brewers' business was important to the T.S. group, for regular consignments had been carried on G.R. vehicles. The new contract was given excellent publicity due to the fact that the vehicles were the new shaft-drive Scammell rigid six wheelers. So successful was the Scammell/C.D.& T. combination, that before long the original contract was increased to take in several of another new product from Watford - the Scammell Rigid Eight.

Probably on the strength of the Whitbread contract, C.D.& T. were able to negotiate a contract with Bulmers the cider manufacturers. This featured vehicles similar to those of the Whitbread type, save that they used Leyland chassis.

Having struggled through the war years with the usual problems of engine and tyre shortages, a replacement fleet of Scammell rigid eights started to appear as soon as they were available, and some were delivered after nationalisation. Soon the Scammells became supplanted by FG Foden and AEC Mammoth Major chassis types, and the brewery contract ended as Whitbread expanded its own fleet.

Originally referred to as Ref:A7 in 1948, the C.D.& T. (Contracts) Ltd, part of T.S. was later listed as A8, then as Unit A52 Contracts. The depot in Power Road, Chiswick still exists.

That part of the T.S. group covering East Anglia was given the rather obvious title of East Anglian Transport Services Ltd, and one can be forgiven for wondering if other member companies in the group might also have been reconstituted had the group remained in private hands after 1947. But the roots of the T.S. group in this area began, like so many others, in the period immediately following the Great War.

It was in April 1920 that a limited company was registered to take over the business of haulage contractors and motor engineers carried on by Child & Pullen at Ipswich. The purchase price was £2100 in shares, the registered office at 1A Portmans Road, Ipswich, and the main business between that town and London, where an agreement was reached with Bernard's Garage located in Hackney Road to act as their London depot.

Under new control Child & Pullen Ltd (C&P) expanded its catchment area to include Clacton, Colchester, Lowestoft and Great Yarmouth by the early 1930s. By the middle of the decade journeys to the Midlands and the North of England was included in the schedules, and the fleet numbered 56 units. With much of its traffic being perishable produce for the London market - its London depot was not far from Spitalfields Market

A new venture of the era was the setting up of a London sales depot for produce located just south of the Thames in Walworth. This fresh side to the business was known as C&P Sales Ltd.

By 1938 another old established haulage business was acquired by C&P, this being the Sudbury (Suffolk) Transport Service Ltd based at Sudbury and Long Melford. Like C&P themselves, this business had been started in 1919, and had gradually increased until, in the early 1930s it was operating six lorries, becoming a limited company in February 1934.

Following the acquisition of the Sudbury-based company C&P was reconstructed as Child & Sons Ltd in 1938, and a fleet total of 100 vehicles was claimed at this juncture. Interestingly, the London depot was now listed as being that of H.& G. Dutfield Ltd.

The area to the southeast was covered by the fleet of Gammon & Dicker Ltd, and they were acquired by TS toward the end of the 1930s. The origins of this part of the group went back to the early part of the century, when Arthur Gammons used small sailing boats to take local produce from Chatham in Kent, up the Thames to service the London markets. He also controlled local collection and delivery in Chatham, by employing a number of horsedrawn carts. The vagaries of tides and wind prompted a change to motor transport in later years, and in 1936 expansion took place by the acquisition of the business of P. L. Dicker, who were based at Southborough also in Kent.

This new company was registered as Gammon & Dicker Ltd on 1st February 1936, with a registered office at Holborn Wharf, Chatham and a capital in excess of £10,000, with a combined fleet of 43 A-licenced vehicles. Directors were listed as Henry Burgess, Graham Burgess, James Nutter, Percy Dicker and David Richardson. Within three years the company was acquired by TS, and only Percy Dicker remained on the board of the new administration.

Upon acquisition by the RHE, the company was designated as A10, with the London office listed as 29 Duke Street, SW1; the Chatham address was the old Holborn Wharf in Medway Street, with a London depot located alongside the railway at Arches 456/460 in Silwood Street, SE16.

Moving our attention to the south coast, we come upon that arm of the TS empire which was located at Brighton. The Southern Transport Company Ltd was established in September 1914, and early business was conducted purely locally, in the Brighton and Hove area, but later a regular service to London was instituted.

Expansion was gradual in the early days of the company, with a certain emphasis being placed on establishing a contract-hire facility. Naturally attention was focused on local businesses, and unusually one important customer was the local Co-operative Society. By the outbreak of war in 1939 some 100 vehicles were listed on their A-licence, but many of these would have been A-contract tonnage. Soon after the end of the war TS took control of the company, and it was not long after this that it passed into RHE hands. Originally listed as Ref:A19, it was later allocated Unit No.A26.

Another old-established and well-known haulier in the London area was Kneller & Chandler Ltd, which had its roots way back in the expansionist years following the 1918 Armistice. Registered as a private limited company in July 1922, with a capital of £2000, the company base was at 25 Wheler Street, E1, close to the City. Traffic was of a general nature, with services to Bristol and Birmingham being its mainstay.

In the mid 1930s Kneller & Chandler Ltd was acquired by TS, by which time depots had been established at Victoria Road, St Phillips, Bristol, and at Butlin Street, Nechells, Birmingham. The fleet details at that time were listed as being eleven Scammell, six Foden and eight Commer, with a total claimed capacity of 240 tons. A reference of 1939 put the fleet at 26; made up of 12 Scammell, nine Foden, two ERF, two Commer and one Thornycroft, with an aggregate tonnage capacity of 260. When it passed into RHE hands the undertaking was listed as A13, later becoming Unit A18 in the Southeast division.

Of more local London tradition, was the fleet of Henry Bayes & Sons, a very old-established business with roots going back to 1879. Naturally the basis was horsedrawn vehicles in the early days, but motor lorries were adopted as the years went by. The proprietors, F.J. Bayes and S.G. Bayes, registered their business as a private limited company in October 1922, with an authorised capital of £20,000. By the time the goods vehicle licensing system was in place, the fleet totalled 39 motor vehicles, plus a number of horsed vans.

In the mid 1930s control of Henry Bayes & Sons Ltd was acquired by TS, and the reconstructed company board still included two members of the Bayes family, although not the two originators.

By this time the fleet had grown to 60 vehicles, with about two-thirds being on the general A-licence and the balance on A-contract, with a reduction in the number of horsedrawn vans. The 1938 return listed the motor fleet as 27 Bedford, 16 Leyland, 14 Commer, 14 Ford, six Chevrolet, two Maudslay and one Dennis, with the registered office being at the TS headquarters in Kingsland Road, while the operating centre was their old address at 87/89, Curtain Road, EC2. Under the reference of A4, Henry Bayes Ltd passed into RHE hands, later being allocated as Unit A2 in 1949.

In middle England, Kinders Garage & Haulage Ltd was established in June 1922, the business having originated just three years earlier. Of the four directors, two were ladies, a feature not commonplace in the rough and tumble of 1920s general haulage.

Under the tough management of Alice M. Walker and fellow director Mrs Bonshor, the company progressed steadily. Under the new Road & Rail Traffic Act of the mid 1930s, 18 vehicles were listed, with a carrying capacity of just over 230 tons. By 1938 the fleet total had risen to 21 and Miss Walker was in sole charge, but in the early part of the next decade a decision was made to join the TS group.

In 1944 the nearby Loughborough Transport Company was acquired by TS, and was duly attached to the Kinder operation with a new title - Kinders Transport Ltd. Under RHE control the operation was listed as A12 with the main address as being Lutterworth Road, Blaby, Leics., plus the old Loughborough Transport depot at Selbourne Road, Loughborough. The latter address was listed in the RHE Gazetteer as having business in indivisible loads, but this was later deleted as RHE business was further rationalised and depots more accurately designated. The handling of such loads was really more suited

to the Pickfords division of the organisation. Both of the Kinders addresses were allocated to Unit E12 in the Eastern division of BRS in 1949.

Much of the work executed by TS group members was in the north of England, and mention has already been made of NWTS who were operating in the northwest part of the country. A somewhat complementary arrangement existed over to the northeast, where the names of Northumbrian Transport Services Ltd and Orrell & Brewster came to be part of the TS empire.

But we must first go back again to the period following the end of the Great War, when in Manchester the Chamber of Commerce had set up a clearing house operation for the benefit of its members. Under the management of Nathan Fine, the facility soon fulfilled the wishes of its members, but it was later floated off as a separate identity and controlled by its past manager, Nathan Fine. Meanwhile, over in Newcastle-on-Tyne, Northumbrian Transport had been set up in 1925 and it soon saw the potential of traffic across the country to and from Liverpool and Manchester. Later services to Glasgow and Hull also ensued.

Other local operators were Atkinson Transport of Newcastle-on-Tyne, with half-a-dozen vehicles, Joynson Loughton & Co. with 10 lorries, and the smaller County Transport of Glasgow, which together had become associated with Orrell & Brewster of Gateshead. By linking all the foregoing operations, TS created Northumbrian Transport Services Ltd with depot facilities at Gateshead, Hull, Manchester and Glasgow. All this activity taking place around 1936. With the advent of the RHE these four locations were given the Ref:A16, but later in 1949 Unit D35 was used to identify them.

A late formation in the grand transport plan of TS, was that of West Midland Roadways which first saw the light of day in June 1945. This last geographically titled operation embraced the haulage companies previously known as Henry Hawker of Burton, H.& S. Hawker of Nuneaton and A.G. Andow of Walsall.

Henry Hawker's haulage business was acquired by TS in November 1937, when a new company H. Hawker (Burton) Ltd was set up with a capital of £30,000 and with about 30 vehicles operating on A-licence. Operating from Brampton Garage, Lichfield Road, Burton-on-Trent, the fleet of tippers and flats was made up of Bedford, ERF, and Leyland types.

The somewhat similarly named H.& S. Hawker Ltd of Tuttle Hill, Nuneaton was registered as a private limited company in September 1937, operating 23 vehicles on A- and B-licences.

The third member of this trio, A.G. Andow & Co.Ltd, was first registered in March 1935. Their 14 vehicle fleet was based at Pleck Garage, Darlaston Road, Walsall, and their A-licence authorised 11 Bedford tippers plus a couple of Guys and a solitary Morris flat. By the time of RHE acquisition, the three locations of West Midland Roadways were designated as A20, but later they were designated as Unit E92.

Another TS member of some repute was that of A.H. Barlow, a Manchester based haulier specialising in long distance transport, notably between the Northwest and London. Originally established in 1920, a private limited company was floated in 1938 with a capital of £9,000, and control passed to TS soon after. A fleet of Guy, Foden and Scammell vehicles comprised the larger outfits, while smaller IHC types did the local work; the fleet totalled 30 in 1938, these running under both A- and A-contract licences.

The Manchester base was at 33/45, Cecil Street, Greenheys, while the London end of the business was located at 18 Marshgate Lane, Stratford, E15. Upon nationalisation, A.H. Barlow (Transport) Ltd was referred to as A3, this later changing to Unit C4.

Another T.S. constituent company was that of S.J. Megenis Ltd, which was incorporated in October 1935 to take over the business of haulage previously carried out by the proprietor, Mr S.J. Megenis from premises in Isabella Street, London SE1. The 1938 register lists the fleet as being 16 A-licensed, plus six on an A-contract licence, including 13 Morris, five Bedford, two Ford, one Singer and one Commer, all with flat, van or tipper bodywork. The date of association with TS is not clear, but it probably dates from the late 1930s, possibly 1938/39. The RHE gazetteer lists the address at Isabella Street plus an address at 44, Mount Street, Southall, Middlesex under the reference A14. By 1949 Unit No.A22 had been allocated to the operation.

A late addition to the activities of the group was that of Bert Whiting, a London-based haulier which probably originated in the 1920s, and being formed into a limited company in August 1932 with a capital of £700. A listing of 1939 gives a fleet total of 18 vehicles, operating on an A-licence granted by the Metropolitan Licensing Authority.

The company joined the TS group in the early post-war period, and provided somewhat of a change in the mode of operation, they being specialists in the field of meat haulage and 'smalls' in the London area. The Whiting depot was located at 98/100 Balls Pond Road, Dalston, E8, a location which was to prove useful as a London terminal for vehicles from other group companies. Upon nationalisation Bert Whiting Ltd was given the reference A22, this later being changed to Unit A13.

W. Bradbrook & Sons was a London-based general haulage company, occupying Arch 294 off Cambridge Heath Road, Bethnal Green. A 1938 listing gives the fleet as including 49 vehicles and 13 trailers. After incorporation, the company passed into TS control during the 1940s, then into the RHE as reference A6, later becoming Unit A4.

RPC Transport Ltd was a TS subsidiary company registered on 23 November 1938 with a nominal capital of £100, for the sole purpose of supplying 27 vehicles on A-contract for the Rugby Portland Cement Co.Ltd. The fleet of flat and dropside lorries was used for the delivery of bagged cement, and included ten Thornycroft, six Commer, eight Leyland, two Foden and one Morris, although within a year it was increased to 34 vehicles. With the proposition of nationalisation looming on the horizon, the Rugby Portland Cement Co. came to an agreement with TS, and acquired the fleet for operation under their C-licence.

J. Blaney Ltd was located at Imperial Garage, Sunderland Road, Felling, Newcastle-on-Tyne, and carried on the business of road transport contractors and automobile engineers. With origins going back to 1889, the transport service had originally been local, but by the 1920s regular services were on Newcastle to Manchester and Liverpool routes.

In the late 1920s the fleet total stood at ten, which included four 4/5 ton Albion flats, three Saurer and trailer outfits, one Leyland 8-tonner, an AEC of 5/6 ton capacity and an open-bodied 30 cwt Chevrolet. In the early 1930s a couple of sixwheel Fords were added, bringing the total to 12. Later in the decade, changes to vehicle fleet took place, but the total remained at a round dozen. A couple of ERF eight wheelers were added, the sixwheel Fords disposed of, and trials made

with Bedford and Dennis types in the 3/5 ton range.

The acquisition by TS is thought to have taken place during the 1940s, but the J. Blaney Ltd fleet was not amalgamated with Northumbrian Transport Services as one would have imagined. We can only conject that this might have taken place later, had not nationalisation come along. Under RHE control, J. Blaney Ltd was given the reference A5, later changed to Unit D9, and a Liverpool address at 15, Paradise Street listed.

Quincey's was a Leicester haulage contractor established in 1924 with an office at 'Quincella', Porlock Street, and a garage at Minehead Street. A change to a limited company took place in November 1931, with an initial capital of £10,000 and a fleet of nine Thornycrofts. A daily service between Leicester and London, and Leicester and Leeds was advertised. By the end of the 1930s three more Thornycrofts had been added to the fleet, and a new address at Anstey Lane, Leicester was listed. It is unclear when the transfer to TS took place, but it was probably in the late 1940s. Quincey's Ltd was given the reference A17 following the take-over of TS by the RHE, it later becoming Unit E17.

EASTERN ROADWAYS

In eastern England there existed a small group of transport companies serving the major towns, of this highly productive agricultural area. Known in the trade as the Eastern Roadways group (ER), this organisation was originally created by J.W. Cook & Co.Ltd, a firm of wharfingers based at 130-135, Minories, London, EC1, who held the majority of the share capital. Established in October 1929 with a capital of £5000 and an office at 30 Great St Helens, London, EC3., Eastern Roadways Ltd's first depot was at Stansted Road, Bishop's Stortford, Essex.

A note of the vehicle fleet in 1934 gives a total of 25, while by 1938 this had risen to no less than 65 units. There were AEC, Albion, ERF, Ford and Scammell types, and a new address of Hall Road, Norwich emphasised the transfer of the company's operation further eastward.

Upon acquisition by the RHE in February 1949, the company was allocated the reference AL1. The London depot at 43a Settles Road, E1., was listed, and the traffic in 'smalls' and general haulage between London and Bury St Edmunds mentioned. By the time the Unit Number system had been established Eastern Roadways was allocated Unit H22 and its area of operations listed as being London to Kings Lynn and Norwich for the London depot. Traffic between Bishops Stortford, Cambridge and London was given for the Bishops Stortford depot, while Norwich was quoted for London traffic only.

Also in the ER group was Day's Transport Ltd of Ipswich, a company formed in June 1935 to take over the haulage business operated by Messrs H.C. and L.B.A. Day from 961, Woodbridge Road, Ipswich. There were 56 vehicles in the fleet which operated under A- and A-contract licences. Upon nationalisation. Day's Transport Ltd was listed as AL4, and a smaller depot at North Station Yard, Victoria Chase, Colchester also listed, which had been the base of another business that Day's had acquired earlier.

Orwell Transport was another Ipswich based company, but it had been absorbed by Day's somewhat earlier. Because of the licensing records it was listed separately as AL5 by the RHE even though it shared the same Woodbridge Road premises.

Suffolk Road Transport was established as early as 1920

with a capital of £2000 and an office address at 1, Out Northgate, Bury St Edmunds, later moving to Station Hill in the same city. A record of 1934 lists just eight vehicles, and the company passed into the ER group sometime in the 1940s. It was allocated Ref:AL8 when acquired by the RHE, and the AQ3 form lists the vehicles as eight Leyland, two Foden, and one each of Ford, Scammell, Bedford and Morris.

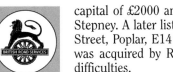

Another company within the ER group was T.C. Grange Ltd, who set up business in 1924, and ten years later had a very mixed fleet which included Maudslay, Thornycroft, AEC, Karrier, Morris, Bedford and Saurer, and all within the total of 201 tons. At the time of nationalisation things had changed somewhat, but there was still variety in that the 35 vehicles included five AEC, six ERF, four Dodge, nine GMC, a Commer and 10 Leyland, one of which was a 1932 machine with a crane. The company, which operated from Quay Garage, Wells, Norfolk, was brought into the ER group by the formation of a limited liability company in July 1935, by which time the fleet total was 27.

In April 1936 Sheringham Haulage Ltd - a 10 vehicle fleet - was registered with a capital of £1600. It was run by three members of the Johnson family. It was later acquired by the ER group, probably in the 1940s, and the depot address was given as being Quay Garage - the home of T.C. Grange.

Two other operators within the ER group were based at Roudham, East Harling near Norwich, these being R.T. Lawrence Ltd and F.W. Riches Ltd. The former was a company incorporated in July 1937 with Roy Trafford Lawrence and George Henry Lawrence as directors, with eight vehicles and eight trailers on A-licence. Little is known of F.W. Riches Ltd, it might have been included within the R.T. Lawrence detail.

Mallon & Grange was a small operator based at Rookery Farm, Swaffham, Norfolk which at the time of nationalisation had a listed fleet of nine Albion, four Dodge, one Morris and one Ford. The vehicles were operated either as flats or cattle trucks, for there were a number of detachable bodies, including two constructed for meat transport.

Another ER group company was that of Robinson's Transport (Beccles) Ltd, which was registered in March 1935 with a capital of £5000. By 1938 the fleet stood at 22 vehicles and six trailers, and the address was listed as London Road, Beccles, Suffolk.

THE DAVIS GROUP

BRS Gazetteer No.9 listed the undertakings acquired up to 31st May 1949, and included in this was the Davis group of companies. Some records mention a group of eleven companies, but information on some of them is rather vague.

The parent company was R. Davis (Haulage) Ltd, which was formed on 26 November 1935 to take over the haulage business established in 1887 by Mr John Davis. The company started with an authorised capital of £10,000 and four directors named as Frank Davis, Abraham Davis, Aaron Davis and Solomon Davis, all brothers. The registered office was at 52/54, High Holborn, WCl, while the company head office was listed as 41, Buckfast Street, E2. A fleet of 31 vehicles operating under an A-licence granted by the Metropolitan Licensing Authority was noted.

A number of other transport companies were taken over by R. Davis, among them being the well known name of Risdon Semper. This company was registered in April 1931 with a

capital of £2000 and an address at 40 Trinity Square, Stepney. A later listing gives an address at 44 Grenade Street, Poplar, E14 when 14 vehicles were operated. It was acquired by R. Davis in 1941, when in financial difficulties.

Another associate company was J.E. Read, an operator mainly serving the Spitalfields vegetable market. It was acquired by R. Davis in 1945 and had 44 vehicles. In the Northwest, T.H. Prince had a small transport operation near Warrington trading as E. Prince & Son. This company was taken over by R. Davis on 31 July 1947. H.H. Jardine was another company acquired, but actual details are lacking. Located in south London it earlier had some Leylands on contract to the Brooke Bond Tea company.

Other companies in the group were listed as being Richard Hacker Ltd., P. Jacobs (Haulage) Ltd., B. Modish Ltd., Ardleys Transport Ltd., Gaults Transport (Warrington) Ltd., and Lovell & Co. Ltd.

At the time of nationalisation there was disagreement between the R. Davis group and the RHE, this continuing until 1954.

The PRO records provide some information on the group, with AQ3 forms for the fleets of R. Davis, J.E. Read, E. Prince & Son, Richard Hacker Ltd., H.H. Jardine and Risdon Semper. From this information we can see that when the group fleet was listed on 1st June 1949 a substantial undertaking was acquired.

The parent company had a mixed fleet of 37 vehicles ranging from 5/6 ton Austin and Bedford trucks, through a couple of Vulcans rated as 7-tonners, plus some Bedford and Leyland 'Lynx' artics and on to modern 'Beaver' and 'Octopus' rigids. A valuation of £38,718 was put on the vehicles.

The Risden Semper fleet of 32 vehicles and nine trailers was valued at £51,830, while the 12 vehicles of Prince were quoted as £10,660. Reed's fleet of 49 vehicles and two trailers, which was made up largely of Austin and Bedford drop-side trucks, plus some Bedford artics and five rigid eight wheelers, was valued at £39,187.

H.H. Jardine's fleet was listed as 12 vehicles and two trailers valued at £12,412, and included four Leylands, two each of Foden and Austin plus one each of AEC, ERF, Bedford and Maudslay marques.

The Prince fleet was made up of seven Leylands, a couple of Fodens, plus an AEC, an Austin and a Bedford. The J.E. Read roster of vehicles shows that it was made up largely of Austin and Bedford dropside trucks for the Spitalfields market traffic, plus a handful of medium weight artics and some four- and eight-wheel Leylands.

The fleet of Richard Hacker Ltd is quoted as being 23 which included eleven Bedford, six Austin, four Leyland, one Seddon and one Maudslay, which were valued at £18,321 in June 1949. No details are listed of vehicles for the other companies, namely Kodish, Jacobs, Ardleys, Gaults and Lovell.

The RHE allocated Unit A104 to the Davis group, and quoted the address of 166/176, High Street, Poplar, E14. Within a short while the Unit address was changed to 53-73, Central Street, EC1, it becoming Bow group.

In November 1950 the vehicles and drivers were re-allocated to East Ham, Monument, Stratford and Millwall groups.

Note: A fourth major undertaking to be absorbed - the important and well-known group of Holdsworth & Hanson and Bouts-Tillotson, will be dealt with in great detail in a separate publication which is currently in the course of preparation.

Left: Displaying an Ex Army Transport Ltd headboard, this 1930 Associated Daimler carries the owners name of J. Cooke & Burgess of Basford, Stoke-on-Trent, one of the many contractors working under the auspices of the transport clearing house. The Ex Army Transport company was one of the founding members of Transport Services Ltd, and in 1942 'E.A.T.' changed its name to North Western Transport Services.

Right: The brilliant sun highlights the streamlined front of this impressive DG6/15 eight wheeler when photographed in Manchester in June 1948. Unusual for a haulage vehicle, no address or telephone numbers are painted on the vehicle, which still retains the wartime white edges to the mudguards. North Western Transport Services Ltd was established in 1942 with a base at Salford.

Below: General Roadways were famous for their fleet of Scammells, the earlier articulated types being upstaged in later years by the splendid rigid eights. This wartime example was photographed in June 1948, and the bright sunshine helps highlight the man-sized fixed starting handle and Gardner decompression lever positioned either side of that impressive radiator. Even the street lamp is worth preserving!

Above: Looking every inch a legendary trunk vehicle, this General Roadways Scammell was typical of the fleet in pre-nationalisation days. Photographed in the rather sombre surroundings near to the Spring Place, Kentish Town depot. Number 70 had probably endured its fair share of long distance journeys. The outfit still retains a workman-like air, and is complete with two mirrors, fog lamp, radiator thermometer and a toolbox on the trailer.

Below: Pictured outside the General Roadways depot in Spring Place, Kentish Town, is one of the rigid eight Scammells loaded and ready to roll. Unfortunately something is amiss, and the fitters are in attendance with their Austin KB8 van JXB683, seen at the rear. The company's fleet colours were green with black wings and gold colour lettering and lining.

Above: The railway arches in Druid Street, SE1 provide the backdrop to this impressive DG Foden twinsteer and trailer of Child & Sons, as it waits to be loaded on this April morning in 1948. This was one of the larger outfits in the Child's fleet, and it had probably made a delivery to one of the produce merchants in the nearby Borough market. Providentially the vehicle carries a fire extinguisher attached to the windscreen centre pillar, and the trailer attendant has been leaning heavily on the nearside cab door rail!

Right: It was a misty winters day in 1947 when this AEC 'Monarch' of Child & Sons was photographed, with its driver busy at the rear untying the sheet. Based at Ipswich, Child & Sons were part of the Transport Services operation entitled East Anglian Transport Services, and this vehicle was one of a trio of AEC four wheelers first registered early in 1947. Disappointingly, the driver has found it necessary to use a piece of wood to wedge up the nearside window!

Right: A trailing axle sixwheeler of Knellers pictured outside a yard which might have been their own premises. This 1938 Foden was one of nine such machines operated in pre-war days, and the DG radiator and cab show the modern streamlined style adopted by that manufacturer. The white-edged front mudguards are a reminder of the dreadful conditions under which these vehicles and their drivers operated in wartime days.

Right: An early post-war example of the Kneller & Chandler fleet is this ERF 7-tonner which is fitted with the diminutive headlamps of the wartime models. Photographed in March 1948, the vehicle stands outside Bedford House in Ford Square E.1. which was close to the Kneller premises in Wheler Street just off Commercial Street.

Below: Photographed close to their premises in Curtain Road EC2, this 1947 O-type Bedford was typical of the Henry Bayes & Sons Ltd fleet, for much of their traffic was for the east London furniture manufacturing trade. The vehicle was probably supplied to the bodybuilder in chassis/scuttle form, for the cab is built integral with the Luton body, and the general layout suggests that a coach chassis was specified.

Right: Parked near the fuel island at Markyate in November 1948 is this Maudslay 'Maharanee' artic low-loader operated by Kinders Transport Ltd. The vehicle was based at the company's Loughborough depot which specialised in heavy haulage, the premises originally being the base of the Loughborough Transport Co., which was acquired by Transport Services in 1944. Note the assortment carried on the trailer swan-neck - spare wheels of differing sizes, packing timber, chocks, storm lanterns, a lorry sheet and of course a manual winch.

Above: Photographed in Edinburgh in July 1948, this Northumbrian Transport Services 1934 AEC is set in a period street scene which includes granite setts and tramlines, together with Maypole Dairies, Timpsons shoe shop and Adairs, the tailors and outfitters.

Below left: The difference in wheel sizes is most apparent in this photograph of a 1942 Scammell rigid eight in the livery of Northumbrian Transport Services Ltd, shown just prior to nationalisation. A Scammell design of tank is carried on the chassis, and this has the large circumferential supporting ring centred over the rear bogie. The front panel of the cab carries the telephone numbers of the Gateshead, Manchester, Glasgow and Hull locations.

Right: Northumbrian Transport Services Ltd was listed as being acquired before September 1948, and yet there is no sign of a BRS crest on this vehicle, which was photographed almost a year later. This Leyland stands in the dock complex at Liverpool, with sheets of waiting for the crane to unload the cases of export goods. The strong frontal lighting shows clearly the hinges for the driver's opening windscreen, a feature of this 1947 Hippo model

Above: R. Barr (Leeds) Ltd are probably less known for their haulage business, than that of the coach operation, which is better known as Wallace Arnold. Barr and Wallace Arnold Trust Ltd was the holding company which controlled both the goods and passenger carrying sides of the business. In July 1949 three of the Barr companies were acquired by the BTC: R. Barr (Leeds) Ltd, W.H. Fish & Son Ltd, and Alf Harrison (Leeds) Ltd, all being located at Saynor Road, Hunslet where the group had a large garage and workshop. The BTC allocated Unit No.D67 to the operation, and announced that other acquisitions would be based on this location. A typical example of the R. Barr fleet is this 1943 model CI5 ERF, photographed in Edinburgh in 1948.

Below: Pictured at the South Mimms traffic lights on its journey northward, this R8 Scammell is typical of the Barlow fleet at the time of nationalisation. By the shape of the sheet, the load could well be a mixed load of beer, for the company carried a wide variety of traffic for return loads on their London-Manchester trunk. Note the mixture of tyres on this vehicle, with giant singles on the rear bogie. Also that spare front wheel could be a bit of a handful to a solo driver!

Right: Bert Whiting & Son Ltd was based at Balls Pond Road N1, and its traffic consisted mainly of meat and 'smalls' in the London area. The photograph shows one of the many Bedfords in the fleet engaged on meat cartage. This O-type carries an aluminium box body with double rear doors, a type much favoured in the meat carrying trade, because of the ease of washing out at the end of the day.

Left: Typical of the parking areas where lorries could be found in our industrial towns in the post-war years, this part of Liverpool shows scars left by wartime bombing. Two of the J. Blaney fleet are parked up on this site not far from Dockhead one lunchtime, while a handful of period coaches are to be seen in the background. Prominent is one of the light 2C14 model ERFs which has a 17'-6" body and was delivered in July 1936.

Right: This 1947 Maudslay Mogul of Southern Transport, displays the utility style of radiator grille adopted for wartime models of the marque. Photographed in May 1948, it is standing in Warwick Street, Brighton and the company premises can be seen in the background. The load of beer casks represents the morning deliveries for one of the Brighton-based brewery companies.

Left: One photograph which underlines the co-operation between Transport Services group companies, is this showing an O-type Bedford of Quinceys Ltd making a call at the Curtain Road premises of Henry Bayes & Sons Ltd, on a dull November day in 1947. Quinceys Ltd was based at Leicester, being established in 1924 and becoming a limited company in 1931. A daily service was provided between the home base and London and Leeds.

Above: Eastern Roadways Scammell No. 409 awaits the return of its driver in Silvertown Way early in 1948, after delivering its load of produce to the docks nearby. The shorter radiator with the outside filler cap used on these 1940s chassis gives them a totally different frontal aspect when compared to the earlier types. This vehicle carries the Hall Road address in Norwich, while others displayed Prince of Wales Road as their legal address.

Right: As with Transport Services, the Eastern Roadways group was a long time user of the Scammell marque in both rigid and artic form. This Rigid Eight is lettered as Suffolk Road Transport, but follows the basic livery and layout of the Eastern Roadways fleet of which it was part. The dropsides are of low height compared with many other vehicles, and even the cab interior is finished in the pale cream fleet colour - a pleasant change from the reds and greens of many hauliers.

Left: This is unfortunately a cut-out style of photograph used for advertising, but it does show the adaptation of the regular Eastern Roadways livery to accommodate a large display for Watney, Combe, Reid & Co, the brewer whose malt was transported in this resplendent ERF eightwheeler. Fleet No. 81 was one of two CI682 model chassis supplied toward the end of 1935, and fitted with lightweight cabs and bodies by Duramin Ltd. One report mentions the fact that Watneys paid Eastern Roadways £100 per annum for the vehicle to be finished with their advertisement!

Above: Unusual among vehicles in the Eastern Roadways group were the cattle trucks in the fleet of Mallon & Grange of Swaffham, Norfolk. The area is mainly agricultural, but not thronged with livestock, so this Albion has been supplied with a platform body with provision for fitting dropsides, or a detachable cattle container as shown here. Notice how this 1946 model Albion carries two fleet numbers - M14 presumably for the local Mallon & Grange operation, but also 418 as a E.R. group number.

Right: The fleet of R. Davis Ltd with their associate companies, was a sizeable one, and included medium weight four wheelers, artics and maximum capacity multi-wheelers. This DG Foden had not been in service long when photographed outside the old Poplar Borough Council offices, close to the company headquarters in Poplar High Street in 1948, for the old style diamond pattern tyres are still a matching set.

Right: J.E. Read (Haulage) Ltd was one of the R. Davis associate companies taken over in 1945. J.E. Read had a long established business in Spitalfields market area operating a large number of horsedrawn vehicles. When the Notice of Acquisition was issued, the fleet stood at 49 vehicles and two trailers, and consisted mostly of Bedford and Austin four wheel rigids, together with half-a-dozen Bedford artics, plus five Leyland Octopus flats, two four wheelers and a couple of 'Lynx' rigids. Typical of the Read fleet and its working surroundings, is this 1947 O-type at work in Spitalfields market in the late 1940s.

Below: Risdon Semper & Co. Ltd was acquired by the R. Davis haulage group in 1941, and at the time of nationalisation in June 1949 the A-licensed fleet was put at 32 vehicles and nine trailers. This 1947 Leyland was one of a number purchased by R. Davis Ltd in the early post-war years, similar vehicles appearing in R. Davis, J.E. Read and E. Prince liveries. The vehicle is pictured in a side street not far from the company headquarters in E14, and the row of prefabricated houses sets the scene for the late 1940s. Barely visible in the distance is the slender spire of All Saints Church, Poplar.

Left: A load of 40-gallon drums weighs down this Leyland 'Beaver' and trailer of E. Prince & Son Ltd, the R. Davis subsidiary based at Warrington. The photograph was taken in the operators home town in July 1949, just a couple of months after acquisition by the BTC, so perhaps that the vehicle bears no BRS markings is not surprising. However, HYU420 does not appear in the list of vehicles acquired under the name of E. Prince, for it is shown as being a vehicle in the fleet of Risdon Semper, another R. Davis subsidiary.

Below: Some of the most spectacular vehicles of the pre-nationalisation era were undoubtedly those of Bouts-Tillotson. This photograph shows one of Foden DG eightwheel box vans employed on trunk operations between the main centres of traffic; it is seen at Nottingham in September 1947. In the earlier days of Bouts Brothers many of the box van were painted in an all-over white which was unusual for the period. With the change to Tillotson ownership vehicles were painted red and cream with gold lettering and lining.

Right: Although not so glamourous as the long distance vehicles, the units engaged on collection and delivery for Bouts-Tillotson were turned out in a livery similar to that of the larger vehicles. Fleet No. 172 was one of a number of little artics feeding the large depot at Waterden Road, Stratford, and these Scammell MH3 tractors were well suited to the task. For use in congested city streets they were ideal, although from the driver's point of view very noisy and none too comfortable.

Right: The London depot of Holdsworth & Hanson Ltd was a modern building located in Seward Street, EC1, a particularly narrow thoroughfare which ran east-to-west, linking Central Street with Goswell Road. The Scammell 3ton mechanical horse shown here was one of a number employed in handling the collection and delivery service of the operation, for they were ideal for the manoeuvring necessary, in many of the streets and alleys which abounded in the City as well as the dock areas.

Left: H.& R. Duncan Ltd was a voluntary acquisition by the BTC, and the company was detailed in the very first list of Acquired Undertakings issued in September 1948. Under reference A1/1 the head office address at Lower Gilmore Place, Edinburgh was given, together with the London branch at Hornsey Road, Holloway, N.7. The JNSN pantechnicon shown here was one of a number operated by the company, which used high capacity vans for its traffic, which was mostly furniture removals. In 1949 the London depot of H.& R. Duncan (BTC) Ltd was moved to Ferry Lane, Tottenham which was more suitable, being close to the furniture manufacturing area. Later in 1949 the company was allocated as Unit B5, and later it became known as 40B Edinburgh group.

Above: David Barrie was an old established carrier, with a history going back to 1871. In pre-war days a fleet of 42 was listed, which included AEC, Leyland and Reo, but this DG Foden dates from 1941. The main base of the operation was at 32 East Dock Street, Dundee, with branches at 26 Eglinton Street, Glasgow and 24 Friern Park, North Finchley in north London.

Right: Greenwood's Transport had its origins in 1933 when Mr. E.B. Greenwood set up his haulage business at Ramsey, Huntingdonshire. Farming and gravel extraction also formed parts of the business. Later the haulage side expanded into London, Kent, Bedford, Derbyshire and the Midlands. At the time of being acquired by BRS, Greenwood's Transport Ltd and its associate companies had around 120 vehicles.

Right: J. Morton & Son Ltd was an early acquisition by the BTC, for it was allocated the reference 01, and appeared in the first list of acquired undertakings, with addresses at Quinton Road, Coventry; Rushey Lane, Tyesley, Birmingham; Mosley Road, Trafford Park; and Klondyke Garage, Millwall, E14. The 1937 AEC 'Matador' shown here, was one of the vehicles based at the famous Klondyke Garage in Millwall, and it is seen parked on the downward slope of Peto Street, with the trolleybus overhead above Silvertown Way in the background. The Coventry and Millwall premises of the company later became Unit E15, Birmingham became Unit E8, Manchester, Unit C27; Coventry later being designated as Group 2E, while Klondyke became 65A Millwall group.

Right: All British Carriers Ltd was created in June 1937 by the amalgamation of William Bater & Sons Ltd, Freeguard Brothers Transport Co., Somerton Transport Co. Ltd and G.C. Wadsworth Ltd. A controlling interest in the company was taken by the Red & White United Transport Ltd group. When acquired by the BTC in 1948 the company was referred to as U1, but under the Unit system it was allocated as G1, later becoming 1G Newport group. The Albion CX model shown here had not been in service long when photographed in Covent Garden market in August 1948, and it has not yet had the 'wheel and lion' emblem stuck over the All British name.

Left: One of the older William Wisely vehicles, this 1933 Leyland 'Beaver' has a locally built cab, and carries headlamps barely larger than the sidelights! Loaded with fabrics in various bundles it stands in a certain Bridge Street on true Scottish granite setts and tramlines, sometime in 1948. Wm. Wisely was one of the companies in the Transport Association group of 50-odd concerns, which were acquired by the BTC in 1948.

Above: Photographed in Bristol in July 1948, this 1933 AEC Mammoth dropside appears to be in good condition for its age. The old-style short radiator, fixed starting handle and tiny headlamps, are the trademarks of its period, and the plain livery is in stark contrast to the eightwheeler of the same company shown overleaf.

The signwriter's art was much in evidence on some of the
H.W. Hawker vehicles, the AEC Mammoth Major being a
prime example. Although the body was enclosed by double
hinged doors at the rear, a rolling shutter was provided on the
nearside for access to the front of the load, for when the
vehicle was used for multiple deliveries. This vehicle is fleet
number 24 and dates from around 1934; the exterior autovac
on the cab quarter panel is worthy of note, being typical AEC
practice for the period.

Right: The Talbot-Serpell Transport Co. Ltd was created in November 1922, to take over an existing transport business that had in excess of 50 vehicles. Many American trucks were operated in the early days of the company including Garford, GMC, Packard and Liberty types. In the mid 1930s the fleet became more British in manufacture, with Thornycroft forming the bulk of the fleet, plus Morris, AEC and Scammell. Bedfords began to appear in the fleet during the late 1930s, and that illustrated is one acquired in the early post-war period. The company was nationalised early in 1949 under the reference AR1, later becoming Unit F13, providing fine facilities for BRS in Reading.

Below: Ashman & Street of Thatcham near Newbury, Berks, carried on a small haulage business, which at the time of operator licensing stood at 32 vehicles on A-licence. In September 1936 a private limited company was formed to take over the business, and the title Thatcham Road Transport Service Ltd adopted, the company thereafter being recognised on the road as 'T.R.T.S.'. Under BRS control the company became Unit F40, and was integrated into Reading group (40F). The 1936 Albion shown was photographed in October 1947, by which time it was beginning to show its age, but it had probably been hard worked during the war period.

Right: The British Motor Wagon Co. Ltd., was a subsidiary of H.& G. Dutfield Ltd, being acquired by them in May 1942. The number of vehicles taken over is not known, but Board minutes mention an unladen weight tonnage of around 30tons. This wartime Austin is lettered for British Motor Wagon Co. but the vehicles operated as part of the Dutfield fleet. The company was given the reference B5 in the initial list of BTC acquisitions, later being listed as Unit A5, then 27A Westminster Bridge group.

Left: B & M Contracts Ltd was a subsidiary company of Broad & Montague Ltd of Blackwall Lane, Greenwich, which was acquired by the BTC in the spring of 1949 and listed as Unit A102. Later the depot was allocated as 5A Blackwall Tunnel group, which embraced the operations of P. A. Carter, Allen and Marshall.

Above: Mack's Hauliers Ltd was registered in November 1934, to take over the business of M. & W. Mack of Covent Garden, who operated a fleet of around 200 vehicles. Acquired by the BTC in the middle of 1950, the business operated from three depots located at Bradfield Road, Silvertown, E16, Carter Street off Eccles New Road in Salford, and Belvidere Wharf, Southampton. Traffic was mixed, but there was a large part of the business in bulk liquids. In the 1940s and 1950s an associate company was Mack Trucks (Britain) Ltd, based at Barking, but this business was not acquired by the BTC. The smart Dodge 6-tonner shown here was one of the fleet of vehicles which was valued at £143,507 at the take-over.

Left: In about 1888 J.R. Munday started a horse cab business and later added other types of horsedrawn vehicles, culminating in a fleet of around 500 which included a London bus route. Many horses were supplied on contract hire, and a motor lorry acquired in 1911. At the time of nationalisation in May 1949 much of the traffic consisted of food and food products, from London docks and factories for delivery to Manchester, Liverpool, Wiltshire, Berkshire and Gloucestershire, as well as the Home Counties and London. The veteran Leyland shown here, was one of the oldest in the Munday fleet when it was acquired. It is a TQ8 model first registered in May 1932, passing to Munday late in 1934. Rated for a 10ton payload, the unladen weight was an incredible 7ton 6cwt.

Above: At the time of nationalisation in May 1949, the J. Reece Ltd fleet included 78 vehicles and 17 trailers, and was valued at £52,308. Of the 36 Leyland chassis included in the total were a number of 'Lynx' rigids and artics, one of the latter being shown here. The BTC form AQ3 shows HYU777 as being an ex WD vehicle dating from July 1945, and being licensed in October 1947. With its Dyson 20ft trailer, the vehicle was rated as having a nine ton payload.

Right: Being primarily a parcels and smalls carrier, McNamara & Co. had a large fleet of light- and medium-weight vehicles engaged on collection and delivery work. The Karrier 'Bantam' 2-tonner pictured here outside the Epworth Street premises, was one of a number purchased at the end of 1938, and it has an austere air by way of a plain painted radiator shell and just one headlamp. In BRS hands the McNamara Karriers were transferred to Unit A3 Bouts Tillotson as part of a parcels services grouping.

Right: Several of the long distance hauliers managed to acquire some of the US Lend-Lease International trucks during the wartime period, including a few by McNamara Ltd. Classified as model KR8R, this 1943 example appears to be in wartime grey primer, although a standard McNamara headboard proves its identity. With a combined unladen weight of 5ton 5cwt, payload was around 9 tons. The vehicle was photographed in Leonard Street EC1 in November 1947 and there have been many changes in the area. Surprisingly the church to the left in Tabernacle Street, still exists.

Above: McNamara & Co. had a reputation for building their own bodywork, as well as modifying older types in order to extend their working lives. They also operated some unusual vehicles in their fleet, the Mercedes-Benz artic illustrated being one of batch purchased in the middle 1930s. Photographed on a foggy day in 1947, this example weighed in at 6ton 8cwt unladen and was rated as a 15-tonner, and gives the appearance of having done its fair share of hard work. Under BRS control, these vehicles were quickly disposed of for they certainly did not conform to any future standard vehicle type.

Above: One facet of BRS that is often overlooked, is the large number of horsedrawn vehicles it acquired from carriers both large and small. Naturally it was the smalls and parcels carriers who were still using horses in the post-war years, alongside those used by the numerous dairies, bakers and coal merchants, in addition to those of the railways. Companies such as Carter, Paterson & Co., and Sutton & Co handed over some hundreds of horses and vans in 1948, and they came together with all the personnel and facilities necessary for their continued operation. Our photograph shows one of the Sutton & Co. single horse vans negotiating Ludgate Circus in the 1940s.

Left: G.L. Baker the haulier was established soon after the Great War, but not incorporated until August 1944. At the time of the BRS take-over in September 1949 the traffic was listed as including timber, paper, fruit and vegetables, and shipping. Of the 67 vehicles and 21 trailers acquired, 50 were on A-licence, 13 on A-contract and two on C-licence, and the fleet valued at £44,300.

Right: There were two main facets of the Carter, Paterson & Co. fleet: medium vans for the collection and delivery function and larger 7-tonners for the trunk runs. This ERF CI5 model was designed for trunk operation and usually worked with a drawbar trailer. Delivered in 1943, it was originally fitted with a 16'9" dropside for general work, but the sides were later removed in order to carry containers if required.

Right: The Fairclough fleet was rather plain in appearance: its vehicles purely functional. The company also carried out the maintenance, repair, bodybuilding and painting of its fleet. The vehicle shown is typical of those used for moving loads of chilled and frozen meat from docks to market or warehouses, the solid tyred trailer dating from steam wagon days. For longer journeys four wheel rigids with drawbar trailers were usually employed, although there were a number of six- and eight-wheel insulated vans.

Left: Dawsons was a subsidiary of T.M. Fairclough, all part of the large group which specialised in meat haulage, although the business included the movement of provisions from the provinces, as well as several valuable contract hire customers. The DG Foden shown was a post-war example of the breed being delivered in 1946, and it was turned out in a mid green with white lettering and a white roof. One interesting detail of the Fairclough fleet was the complex numbering system adopted, which consisted of a varying mix of letters and numbers. In this case D.FODE 4 is self explanatory, but some of the other codes were less straightforward.

Above: The fleet of E.R. Ives was listed for take-over in April 1950, and showed 34 vehicles and seven trailers which were valued at £21,195. Thirty-two of the vehicles were on A-licence, with one on a B-licence and the breakdown truck on a 'C'. E.R. Ives Ltd was incorporated in April 1931 to take over the transport business of Mr. E.R. Ives, who disposed of his shares in 1937. The majority shareholding was the Great Yarmouth Shipping Co. Ltd which was a subsidiary of the General Steam Navigation Co. Ltd, but D.F.C. Fairclough held over a third of the shares, and E.R. Ives Ltd operated as part of the T.M. Fairclough group. Traffic was mostly in smalls, with a major part of the business being in the Norfolk, Suffolk and Ipswich areas. Under BRS control the Norwich depot was attached to 1H group. T.M. Fairclough was responsible for the bodywork and painting of vehicles, and the photograph shows one of two Foden eightwheelers in the Ives fleet outside the bodyshops in Christian Street, E1 after painting. A nice touch arranged by Faircloughs, was that when the vehicle was photographed the driver was included!

Left: Matthews & Co. Ltd of 159 Blackfriars Road, SE1 was an old established firm of cartage contractors specialising in meat haulage in London, with a history going back to horse and cart days. Later the company ran a sizeable fleet of Foden steam wagons, and its vehicles were much in evidence around the Central Meat Markets and at the Royal group of docks. The Scammell mechanical horse was to prove invaluable for the work of ferrying chilled meat carcasses twixt dock and market, and this 1948 photograph shows a pair of these vehicles as converted to drawbar trailer operation.

Above: Airlandwater Transport Co. Ltd was originally established in 1921, working locally in north Hertfordshire and gradually increasing their territory toward London as well as further northward. This 1948 photograph shows a Commer 6-tonner of the company, and it displays the telephone numbers of the facilities at Bishops Stortford, Peterborough and Epping. Upon nationalisation the head office and depot at Bishops Stortford was allocated Unit H31, while the depot at Fengate, Peterborough became H56. This vehicle, fleet No.604, cost £980 when bought late in 1947, and the unladen weight was 2ton 7cwt.

Right: H.G. Currell & Co. Ltd of 229 Hatfield Road, St. Albans, was acquired in the first quarter of 1949 and allocated as Unit A89. Not long after, Currell & Rand of Victoria Street were added to the Unit together with a depot in Sutton Road, St. Albans. A fleet of about a dozen vehicles had been operated by H.G. Currell in pre-war days, this 1935 AEC dropside being one.

Right: The Express Transport Service (Wellingborough) Ltd was the title adopted in 1933 for a business operated by Messrs Bates & Harrison of Compton Road, Wellingborough. Acquired by Pickfords as an addition to their parcels business, it became part of the Carter, Paterson and Pickfords Joint Parcel Service just after the war, passing into BRS Parcels Unit A34 initially, prior to transfer to Midland division in 1950. The Bedford van shown is a late WT type which utilised the older type of cab, but incorporated the 1939 style grille. The mixture of headlamps is not standard practice, and probably dates from wartime blackout days.

Right: Mr. A. Peck established his carrying business in 1896, and the first motor vehicle was purchased some 20 years later, enabling a wider area of operation. Following the acquisition of Bert Scroxton in 1934, a combined limited liability company was formed as P. X. Ltd which survived until the BTC take-over in 1950. In the mid 1930s the fleet was divided between depot vehicles and trunk vehicles, with Morris-Commercials in London, Bedfords in Leicester, Fords at Rushden and Leylands for trunk work. Later the fleet became predominantly Austin and Dodge in the medium weight range, with AEC and Leyland as the heavier machines.

Right lower: Langley & Wootton Ltd of Coventry was incorporated in March 1931, and was under the control of Alfred & Hilda Langley and Eunice & George Wootton, with a history going back to steam wagon days. Traffic had included flour, car engines and dock work, but latterly furniture for prefabricated houses and work for the Ferguson tractor plant. In pre-war days a number of ERF four- and six-wheelers worked in the fleet, but in post-war years the JNSNs were purchased because their long bodywork was ideal for carrying tractors. The vehicle shown was a 1947 machine, photographed at Markyate in November 1948, well before the company passed into BRS hands.

Left: Watson Brothers (Burton-on-Trent) Ltd was incorporated in April 1938 to take over the haulage business run by T. and E. Watson, from Fleet Garage, Lichfield Street, Burton-on-Trent. Around 40 vehicles were operated on A-licence, including ERF, Maudslay and Bedford types. This 1945 OW-type still retains some of its wartime white paint.

Below: Photographed in Glasgow on a wet July day in 1948, is this recently delivered 14B1 'Beaver' in service with Ernest Davis (Handsworth) Ltd. There had been several titles to this transport operation, it being known as Grant Davis at one time as well as E & M Davis. The BTC took control about the middle of 1949, and allocated reference E79 for the Holyhead Road address, plus others at Manchester Street, Aston and Whitemore Street. Traffic was general haulage, with a long list of destinations from Glasgow to Southampton.

Right: Unit D128 was allocated to the haulage operations of George Crow & Son (Haulage) Ltd of 177, Thornton Road, Bradford when the company was acquired by BRS, and later becoming 43D South Bradford group. Much of the traffic handled was for the woollen trades located in the area, and the bodywork of this wartime Commer reflects the loads carried. Maximum body space is achieved by the provision of an over cab and bonnet platform, supported by steel bars running down to a channel steel bumper bolted to the chassis front end. With the load in place, ropes would be attached to the front extension supports, placed over the load longitudinally, and pulled taut by means of the ratchets at the rear of the body.

Below: W.H.L. Ford established his haulage business around 1926, and created a private limited company in April 1932 with £500 capital. At the time of its nationalisation in 1949, the fleet included seven Leyland, one Maudslay, one Bedford and a little 5cwt Morris 8 service van, plus four trailers. The vehicles were valued at £5602, and the total compensation was just over £24,000, which includes buildings and loss of business. This wartime photograph shows No.11 in the fleet, a 1936-registered Leyland 'Octopus', with a sizeable load for the Ministry of Food. Wartime lighting regulations can be gauged by the offside headlamp being masked, the nearside one having the bulb removed, and a small spotlight being mounted high up.

Left: R. Keetch & Son Ltd was acquired early in 1949, given the reference A23/3, later becoming Unit E139 together with J. Keetch of Comery Avenue, Seaton of Waterway Street, W. Clark of The Wells Road and Thorneywood Lane, all in Nottingham. A reference of 1939 lists the Keetch fleet as being a total of 24 vehicles on A-licence (East Midlands L.A.), including AEC, Albion, ERF, Bedford, Leyland and Scammell in the 12-15ton load bracket. The AEC eightwheeler shown here at South Mimms traffic lights, was heading north with a load of sawn timber when photographed in 1949.

Left: One of the large transport fleets which was not very conspicuous in its operations, was that of Foulkes & Bailey Ltd of Trafford Park. Since its inception in 1928, the company concentrated on supplying vans on contract hire, and the wartime Bedford seen here was obviously working on the Thos. Hedley contract. Although only three years old when photographed, the van body looks decidedly the worse for wear, although it might well have been transferred from an earlier chassis, and post-war shortages may have prevented extensive repairs. Foulkes & Bailey did not confine their operations to the Manchester area, for they operated from branches in Birmingham, Liverpool, Leeds, Cardiff, Southampton, Glasgow and Bristol.

Right: The Gerrard family had a transport business going back to 1914, and a limited company was created in 1935: Gerrards Transport Ltd. The pre-war fleet was mainly Foden, but the Maudslay eightwheeler illustrated was a 1941 model 'Mikado', which joined the 19 vehicle fleet, and operated on contract to Joseph Adamson Ltd. Under BRS control the Gerrard fleet was allocated as 64C Wentworth group, and this vehicle became 64C415.

Left: One of the smaller vehicles in the Joseph Nall fleet. This 1939 Leyland 'Lynx', photographed in Liverpool in June 1948, certainly looks as though it has earned its keep. The company of Joseph Nall & Co. Ltd was registered in February 1907, although the business was established in 1845. Based in Manchester with branches at Bolton, Moses Gate, Bury, Chorley, Church, Darwen, Hindley, Hull, Liverpool and Wigan, the company were cartage agents for the London, Midland & Scottish Railway Co. During the 1930s the LMSR acquired a controlling interest in the company, and at the outbreak of war the fleet stood at 120 vehicles and trailers plus 700 horsedrawn vehicles!

Left: Hutchinson's Garages Ltd was taken over in the third quarter of 1949, becoming Unit A197, and this rather well-worn 10 ton Leyland 'Steer' found itself allocated to Bermondsey group and numbered 6A268. Hutchinson's had an operating base at Newton-le-Willows in Lancashire, a town on the first passenger carrying railway in the world, with a London depot at Peckham and another at Strood in Kent.

Left: C.S. Walker (Hauliers) BTC Ltd, was given the reference B4 when first listed in September 1948, it being part of the H.& G. Dutfield group. With a depot at Marquis Street, Liverpool the company carried out local work as well as providing connections to the group depots in Manchester and London. Originally designated as B4 the depot was later allocated as Unit C44, then passing on as part of 4C East Liverpool group.

Left: The cranes and sheds on Liverpool dockside provide an authentic background to this OSS model Bedford artic of A.E. Handscombe & Co. Ltd. as it waits to leave with a part load. Started in 1920, the business became a limited company in March 1927 under the directorship of Albert Edward Handscombe, and a capital of £2000.
By the end of the 1920s services covered Liverpool and the surrounding area mostly but with journeys to North Wales, The Potteries, Cheshire, Shropshire and Staffordshire according to demand.
With voluntary acquisition the company title changed to Handscombe Transport (BTC) Ltd, later being allocated Unit C38.

Stevenson Transport Ltd was incorporated in June 1930 with a capital of £5000. By the time goods vehicle licensing was introduced a fleet of 20 vehicles was listed under an A-licence granted by the North-Western Traffic Area, this rising to 28 vehicles and 24 trailers by 1939. Acquisition by the BTC took place in October 1948, and the address listed as 121 Thingwall Road, Liverpool, with a branch at Rowditch Place, Derby. A later edition of the RHE Gazetteer records the address as being 76 Sefton Road, Liverpool (Unit C30) as shown on the cab of this DG Foden ETJ203 photographed in 1948.

Below: Harry & William Beaumont started as carriers and motor engineers, at Chapel Field Works, Ripponden in 1920. In 1930 the business was put on a more substantial footing by the creation of a private limited company - Beaumont Brothers (Halifax) Ltd, and by the mid 1930s 22 vehicles were listed. Further expansion took place, and by the outbreak of war services to Glasgow, Edinburgh, London, Birmingham, Liverpool, Leicester, Manchester and Leeds were advertised, and the company had branches in Glasgow and Birmingham. Voluntary acquisition by the BTC came about toward the end of 1948, the company being classified as Unit D6, later 41D Ripponden group. The 1937 Albion shown bears the inter-linked double B, which the company used as their logo, it being repeated on the radiator grille. A nice period touch is the wartime MWT number, which is still shown on the cab of No.7.

Left: Bennetts' Haulage Co. Ltd, of Liverpool was acquired by the BTC during the first quarter of 1949, and allocated as Unit C85, later passing into 2C Central Liverpool group together with the Liverpool Warehousing & Wharfage Co. Ltd. A very mixed fleet was operated, handling general goods from the many docks, wharves and warehouses around the Mersey. This 1938 WTL Bedford was one of the smaller vehicles in the fleet, and the general dusty appearance of the vehicle and the old sack barrow on the roof, suggest that flour or something similar had been carried.

Below: One impressive fleet taken over in the north-west, was that of W.H. Bowker of Blackburn, Lancs. The company were long-time users of the Leyland marque, and this photograph shows two widely differing types. The photograph is dated 25 September 1949, whereas the take-over date was stated as being some two months earlier, and there is no evidence of BRS ownership. The 'Octopus' on the left was first registered in July 1936, and at the time of the take-over was listed as being a 15ton payload machine with an unladen weight of 6ton 6cwt. On the right is a petrol engined 'Lynx' of 1939, which was rated as a 5½ton load carrier with a licensing weight of just 2½tons.

Left: Blythe & Berwick (1928) Ltd was registered in May 1928 in order to carry on the business of haulage contractors and repairers, after the liquidation of another business which had included bus operation, With an authorised capital of £10,000 the new company had two directors, Philip and Mrs Annie Blythe, with a registered office at 23 Charles Street, Bradford. In the 1930s the Yorkshire Licensing Authority granted an A-licence for 30 vehicles, this being increased to 42 vehicles and ten trailers. In June 1949 the company was acquired by the BTC, becoming Unit D90.

Below: For sheer bulk, this AEC and trailer outfit of Joseph Hanson & Son Ltd takes some beating. By using the maximum permissible length of body, together with an over-cab extension, plus the facility of a flexible height made possible by the open-top, the vehicle really exploits every cubic foot of space. Even the trailer could be used to its maximum, for it was really just a huge cage with an open roof, and a giant, all-enveloping sheet to protect the load from the weather. This vehicle was used on the regular trunk runs between Huddersfield and London, but Joseph Hanson also ran regular services to Glasgow, Edinburgh, Birmingham, Liverpool and Leicester. The Huddersfield depot became BRS Unit D19 in 1949, later group 42D.

Right: Looking rather travel stained and showing signs of refuelling, one of the maximum capacity parcel vans in the I.W. Holdsworth fleet pauses at the South Mimms traffic lights en route to Halifax. I.W. Holdsworth Ltd was one of the companies acquired by the BTC right at the outset of nationalisation in 1948, being allocated as Unit D24, later group 40D. This vehicle was later transferred to Dewsbury/Batley group and became 46D61.

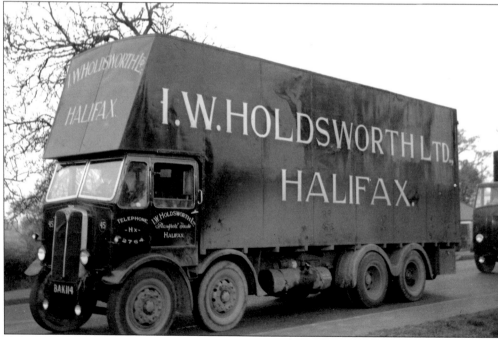

Above: J. Webster (Bradford) Ltd was first registered in November 1933, with an address at Edderthorpe Street, Bradford. The company was later taken over by Blythe & Berwick (1928) Ltd, and the two companies were both acquired by the BTC in June 1949. When control passed to BRS J. Webster had 13 vehicles and Blythe & Berwick 42 lorries. It marked the end of 53 years in transport by Mr. Philip Blythe who had been at the head of the company. The OW-type's livery compliments that of the parent company.

Left: This parcels van is rather unusual in being a semi-forward control Morris-Commercial, and even rarer with its coachbuilt cab. The driver probably had a van boy to look out for him, because with no nearside mirror and no direction indicators, regaining the nearside of the road could be quite an experience! Queen Carriage Co. Ltd was first registered in May 1925 with a capital of £3000, and was based in Huddersfield. As part of the Holdsworth & Hanson group it passed to BRS in 1948 and became Unit D41.

Left: City Express Motors Ltd had its origins way back in 1920 as a parcels carrier. By the mid 1930s some 17 vehicles were licensed, and it was then acquired by Bouts-Tillotson. The fleet total was given as 28 at the end of the 1930s by which time it was part of the Holdsworth & Hanson group. This photograph shows a 1945 Dodge engaged on collection and delivery work, just after the BRS take-over when the letters BTC had been added to the company title.

Left: Although there were many British lorry manufacturers in pre-nationalisation days, we must not forget that for many years before WWII there was plenty of competition from imported truck makers. The war period saw welcome imports in the shape of American trucks for use on the Home Front as well as abroad. This well-loaded IHC K8 model artic, in service with Butterwick & Walker of Leeds, was photographed when parked up near the Beacon cafe at South Mimms, and is a reminder of those days. None of us will envy the driver, for it was no mean feat to sheet and rope a load such as this. Every rope hook has been used, but there are still a couple of spare sheets in the rack slung beneath the sagging Fruehauf trailer.

Below: A fine example of a DG rigid eightwheel Foden in the colours of Fred Cook (Transport) Ltd, snapped whilst parked in a London suburban street sometime in 1948. The sombre row of Victorian terraced houses have somehow managed to retain their iron railings, probably because they protect open sub-basements, but the complete row is holed where one house has been demolished by enemy action. Foden No. 44 stands proudly on a set of 40x8s, while the low-set sun picks out every detail of this archetypal haulage machine of the pre RHE era. The 15 tonner first entered service in December 1946, and is recorded as having an unladen weight of 7¼ tons.

Right: This pair of DG Foden twin steers are parked with other vehicles in the shadow of the impressive Royal Liver Building on Liverpool's waterfront. The insignia on the cab door shows B&F Ltd, or Barrick & Fenton Ltd, and there is some lettering on the cab quarter panel though it is in such poor condition. Barrick & Fenton Ltd, incorporated in March 1936, was closely associated with A. Norman Annison Ltd and Mansell's Motors Ltd, and was located at Hyperion Street, Hull with branches at Yorkshire Garage, Cambridge Street, Birmingham and 30 Chapel Street, Liverpool. Barrick & Fenton, together with its associated companies passed into BRS early in 1949, later becoming Unit D53.

Left: A fine looking Maudslay 'Maharanee' tractor unit, coupled to a bow fronted Scammell trailer, forms this Fred Cook combination pictured unloading at the company depot in Druid Street, SE1 in August 1948. The load make-up is interesting showing as it does the wide variety of goods which went to make up a trailer load for a general haulage vehicle. The Maudslay entered service in October 1947 and was powered by the normal fitment of an AEC six cylinder engine, while the 24ft trailer took the unladen weight up to 7ton 8cwt.

Right: With the tailboard down and the nearside cab door open, the driver was not far away from this Ryburn United 1945 Bedford seen working in Newcastle-upon-Tyne. The livery is the familiar red and cream of the Holdsworth & Hanson group, of which Ryburn United Transport Ltd was a part. Originally known as Ryburn Garage & Transport Co. Ltd., the company was formed in October 1920, changing to Ryburn United Transport Ltd in February 1932, and becoming part of Bouts-Tillotson in 1934, itself taken over by Holdsworth & Hanson the following year.

Above: Adam Atkinson & Co. Ltd of Birtley, Co. Durham, was acquired by BRS toward the middle of 1949, and allocated as Unit D139. The depot was listed as being at Dean Road, Ferry Hill and was included in the BRS category of being able to supply all necessary facilities for BRS vehicles, including fuel, garaging, servicing, repairs, and heavy recovery by night and day. The 1945 Commer artic shown here is of the wartime pattern, and one wonders if it suffered from overheating, for the bottom of the radiator grille has been modified and it has been found necessary to fix a temperature gauge to the radiator filler cap!

Right: Photographer Philip Hine obtained a scoop in July 1948, when he caught this 1937 Beardmore of London Scottish Transport Co. at work in Manchester, where the company had premises at Cheetham Hill. The company was acquired toward the middle of 1949 and allocated as Unit B120, with 286 Clyde Street, Glasgow C.1. as the main address, plus a depot at Armour Street, E.1. There were branches at Aintree Road, Liverpool; South Fort Street, Leith; Silwood Street, SE16 in London; Langley Green, Birmingham; Riverside Garage, Alloa, and Main Street, Doune near Stirling.

Left: The Tyne Ferries & White Star Transport Co. Ltd. (TF&WS), was acquired by BRS at the beginning of 1949, with premises at Mosley Street and Fish Quay, Newcastle-on-Tyne. Originally detailed under the reference Al/l it later became known as Unit D52, then formed into 1D Central Newcastle group in the Tyne/Tees district. Business was described as being general haulage, lighterage and storage, with services to Liverpool, Manchester, south Wales and Tees-side. The 1938 ERF shown here, was photographed on the Tyne quayside in July 1948.

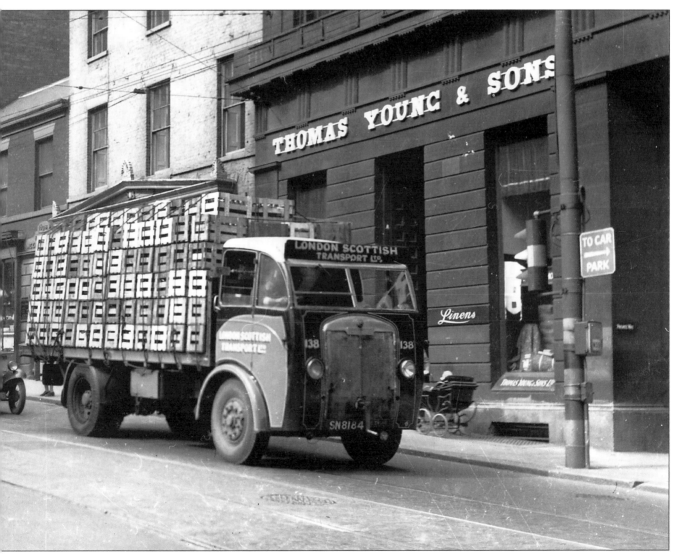

Right: Regal Transport was a member of the National Association of Furniture Warehousemen and Removers because of their furniture moving business, but being regular carriers between Glasgow and London they fell foul of the BTC and were acquired. The Regal vans were distinctive because of their bright livery, and the company employed many AECs. The 'Matador' van shown here was a 1946 machine, and the integral cab has undergone unusual treatment by the bodybuilder, resulting in an almost vertical windscreen. BRS allocated Unit B60 to the company, which had premises in central Glasgow and at Cheshire Street E2 in London.

Below: Conveniently parked outside the company premises in Elliot Street, Glasgow is this Albion of The A.C.S. Motors Ltd, and with the sheet off we can see how the load is stacked. The A.C.S. Motor Co. was registered in November 1922, being formed to take over the business previously carried on by Robert Anderson & Co. with the directors named as R. Anderson and G. Calder. A listing of the mid 1930s mentions that services were mostly around Glasgow and Edinburgh, and that 23 vehicles were operated under an A-licence. Vehicle makes operated included a few Ford and Chevrolet trucks, but the majority were Albions. Sometime during the 1930s a change of title was made to The A.C.S. Motors Ltd, at which time W.G. Stewart became a director. Under BRS control from April 1949 it was allocated Unit B65.

Left: One of the heavier Scammell Mechanical Horse 6-ton artics, this 1937 unit in service with Cowan & Co. of Glasgow, stands in front of a Dennis 'Max' of the same operator. Acquired by the BTC toward the middle of 1949, Cowan & Co. was at first classified as BA1, later becoming Unit B27, with three addresses in Glasgow and a listing of regular trunk services to Manchester, Liverpool, Derby, Birmingham, London and Yorkshire. A Manchester depot was located at Chester Road, Cornbrook.

Above: The Glasgow Hiring Co. Ltd. operated a wide range of vehicles including heavy haulage outfits, general haulage vehicles and vans on contract hire. This well kept Scammell, with its knock-out drop-frame trailer, is seen parked outside the company premises in Glasgow in the late 1940s. The company had its origins back in 1900, and was incorporated as early as 1909. A report of 1929 gives the fleet as 30 vehicles, including Halley and Thornycroft lorries, plus Daimler, GMC and Talbot vans. The fleet doubled in size over the next few years, and by the time goods vehicle licensing was introduced, an A-licence for 80 vehicles was granted. By the outbreak of war in 1939, a total of 130 vehicles was listed.

Left: The majority of vehicles in the Wordie group were in the medium weight range, with Albion and ERF being widely used. This 1943 model CI5 was a 13'11" wheelbase model with an 18ft body by Jennings to Wordie's specification. The driver appears very proud of his vehicle, having added a mascot and coat of arms to the radiator.

Above: The Wordie subsidiary vehicles were turned out in a manner similar to those of the parent company, as shown by this Albion displaying the name of South Western Transports Ltd. It is pictured outside a local haulier's office in Liverpool, probably waiting for a return load, in June 1948.

Right: One of the best remembered Scottish carriers is undoubtedly Youngs' Express Deliveries Ltd, which operated a large fleet mainly in the south of Scotland, with services southward to depots in Manchester, Birmingham and Wigan. Formed in April 1936, Y.E.D. as it was often referred, brought together Scottish Express Deliveries Ltd., Amalgamated Scottish Utility Ltd., Farmers' Traffic Ltd and Majestic Transport Co. Ltd. Depots were established at Paisley, Largs, Ayr, Kirkcaldy and Leith in Scotland, with the head office being at the associate bus operation Youngs' Bus Service at Paisley. Acquisition by the BTC took place in the autumn of 1948, with Y.E.D. listed as providing, from Glasgow, regular trunk services to Abington, Edinburgh, Aberfeldy, Kirkcaldy, Peebles, Aberdeen, Dundee, Manchester, Wigan, Birmingham and London. Originally listed as Unit B18, the Glasgow operation became Scottish Parcels 61B group.

Above: The CX27 model twinsteer Albion was certainly an impressive haulage vehicle, and the front overhang is emphasised by the cut-away of the cab front, which reveals the chassis front end, crash bar mounting, front towing bracket, and steering drop arm and push rod. Vehicle EYS821 was a 1947 delivery to the Holdsworth & Hanson group, being allocated to the Glasgow branch of the organisation. The fact that the vehicle is properly painted and lettered with the (BTC) title, suggests that it was prepared this way when new, for Holdsworth & Hanson was one of the first groups to be acquired early in 1948.

Below: The Dumfries & Galloway Transport Ltd was absorbed into the Wordie group in the late 1930s, and remained as the local depot of the parent company. Dumfries & Galloway Transport became Unit B4 after BRS acquisition, and this 1940 Albion presumably followed suit. The rather plain Wordie group livery is enlivened by just a company title and fleet number, while the mismatched headlamps do nothing to enhance the vehicle's appearance.

Right: A real haulage vehicle in typical working condition, best describes this impressive 1947 Maudslay 'Mustang' twin-steer of Carroll of Cumbernauld. The company ran a small fleet handling traffic mostly in the local area, with a facility at Luton for any goods toward London. They were taken into BRS early in 1949 and allocated as Unit B113.

Below: With its plain black radiator grille and tiny headlamps, this 1947 Maudslay 'Mustang' shows its wartime design features, although it still exudes the air of a real transport machine. The twin-steer layout was always rare enough to demand a second glance, particularly when complete with a drawbar trailer. The Scottish branch of Holdsworth & Hanson was based at Warrock Street, Glasgow which replaced older premises acquired when the company took over Wylie & Lochead in 1935. Under BRS control the depot was listed as Unit B21, providing regular trunk services to Edinburgh, London, Leeds, Manchester, Halifax and Huddersfield.

Right: Photographed in Leith in July 1948 when about a year old, this 0386 model AEC 'Mammoth Major' was the last to be purchased by George Paterson & Sons Ltd of Haddington, East Lothian. The company dated back to 1916 and concentrated on haulage in the Haddington, Leith and Edinburgh areas and provided a regular service between villages in the area and Glasgow. The fleet was a mixed one with vehicles covering capacities up to 15tons capacity, when taken over by BRS in the first quarter of 1949. The company was listed as Unit 44B with regular trunk runs to Glasgow and Edinburgh, and later becoming 44B East Lothian group.

Left: Still bearing its wartime MWT number, this period Albion appears to be ready to move off, while the driver waits for the photographer to make his exposure. The sturdy 1935 model carries a considerable load of Bowater newsprint, and the rolling load appears to be secured by just a few strands of rope at the rear. Mutter, Howey & Co. Ltd was created in June 1919 to take over an older business of railway cartage agents and carriers, based in Edinburgh. Allocated as Unit B19 under BRS control, the company had branches in Aberdeen, Dundee, Dunfermline, Leith, Galashiels, Hawick, Kelso, Kirkcaldy and Selkirk.

One could be forgiven for thinking this photograph was specially posed. With the turreted station building, the railway track recessed into granite setts, the old Albion, and above all that 'wee bairn' studying the Royal Mail Lines poster. Well it just turned out that way for photographer Philip Hine, when he decided to record one of the James Walker vehicles at Dundee Tay Bridge station in August 1947 - pure magic!

Right: The company of Mutter, Howey & Co. Ltd. dates back to June 1919 when it was formed to take over the carrying business operated under a similar title. The main thrust of the business was as general contractors and railway cartage agents, they later acting for the southern Scottish area of the London & North Eastern Railway Co. A fleet of around 50 vehicles was operated, the BTC take-over being in the Spring of 1949.

Below: The Aberdeen-based haulier Charles Alexander was a longtime user of the Leyland marque, and this 'Octopus' was one of a number of post-war machines operated. The company were well placed to handle large quantities of fish landed at the east coast port, and their vehicles undertook long overnight journeys southward, in spite of fierce competition from the railways. In BRS hands the Alexander depot at Old Ford Road was allocated as 2B Aberdeen group. Note the emergency tow bar - an Alexander feature.

Right: Members of the Callander family ran a sizeable transport business in the town of Forfar, converting it into a private company in January 1938. From the Roberts Street premises a fleet of over 50 vehicles was employed on general haulage, agricultural and timber haulage. In the autumn of 1949 the company passed into the control of the BTC, which allocated Unit B30 to the undertaking, it later being operated as 21B Angus group. Number 7 in the fleet was this tough looking DG Foden, which stands on the weighbridge with its load of logs which unusually are not spruce or fir.

Left: James Sutherland began his carrying business in 1876, handling sand, gravel and fish. In 1906 the first steam vehicle was used, and the first motor lorry was bought in 1915. A limited company was created in 1932, and by 1939 there were 44 lorries in the fleet. When nationalisation came in 1951, the fleet was up to 90 vehicles, with much of the business being in fish, timber and canned goods. Under BRS control the operation was titled Peterhead & Fraserburgh group and included vehicles from Wm. Wiseley, French and Eddie. Pictured here are a couple of James Sutherland OW-type Bedfords, set in a scene of granite setts and trawler nets, and they probably carried local fish catches.

Left: Located high up in the north-east of Scotland, W. French & Sons was based at Broadsea Stables in Albert Street, Fraserburgh, operating a mixed fleet on A- and B-licences. A fleet list of 1939 included one International, and their liking for American trucks is reflected in this early post-war GMC photographed in Forfar in July 1948. The left-hand drive truck featured tiny wartime style headlamps and a well placed mirror to help the nearside driving position. The under-seat petrol tank is a reminder of a previous age. The company was acquired during the first half of 1949 and allocated as Unit B110, later joining other local operators to form the 3B Peterhead-Fraserburgh group.

Below: With baulks of timber chocking the wheels of the old solid-tyred trailer, the Rudd Scammell 'Pioneer' AJD140 awaits the return of its crew before proceeding with a Hackbridge transformer. E.W. Rudd was a very old-established haulage contractor specialising in meat and heavy haulage tasks, with steam being used from around 1904. Although both meat and heavy haulage were classed as special traffics by the BTC, Rudd was nationalised, and the fleet passed into the hands of Pickfords.

Bottom: The 1951 Festival of Britain Exhibition would not have been possible without road transport, and BRS was responsible for many movements both during the construction and delivery of exhibits. In this BICC photograph, some of the girders for the Skylon feature of the exhibition, pause in High Wycombe while en route from Hereford to the South Bank site. An ex Burgoine vehicle from Hayes depot handled the load, and here a photographer chats to the driver whilst the trailer attendant attempts to assist following traffic.

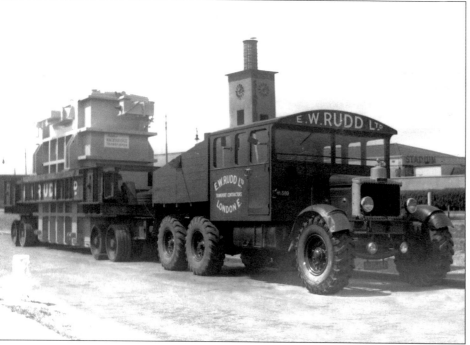

Above: The twin facades of the Royal Exchange and The Bank of England form an imposing background to this scene, which is generally referred to as just 'The Bank', probably because of the London Underground station of that name. The vehicle is a wartime Atkinson sixwheeler of the H. Burgoine fleet from Hayes, Middlesex; the company passed into BRS hands in 1950, their depot at Springfield Road becoming home to 48A Hayes group.

Left: Tuff & Hoar Ltd had its beginnings way back in 1900 at Woolwich in south-east London. By the mid 1930s the motor fleet stood at some 40 vehicles, rising to over 60 by 1939. The company was acquired by the BTC toward the end of 1948, being listed as Unit A31, later becoming group 3A North West Kent. The Ford 7V dropside illustrated was typical of the Tuff & Hoar fleet, although this particular vehicle appears to have a non-standard coachbuilt cab for some reason. The location appears to be somewhere in south-east London, with a wooden cafe standing on a large bombed site where once stood the Royal Oak public house, alongside the London Transport conduit tram tracks.

Right: A photograph which shows an almost archetypal vehicle, used in the countless fleets of individual transport contractors in the days before nationalisation. The production Austin, Bedford, Commer, Dodge and Ford chassis were equipped with a dropside body and perhaps loose tilt cover, and put to work on all kinds of tasks. This example was photographed in November 1948 soon after Gamman & Dicker had passed into BRS hands. Unusually, this vehicle had been transferred to Pickfords, and their fleet number can be seen on the door.

Left: Blands Ltd of Leicester was established during the 1920s and operated services to Leeds, Liverpool and London from its base at Wigston Fields. At the time of operator licensing, the base was listed as Frog Island, and the fleet was up to 22 in number. Nationalisation of the company took place early in 1949, when it was allocated Unit E93, later passing into 42E Leicester Parcels group. The wartime Bedford OX model tractor shown, was registered in 1942, and in this 1949 photograph displays some well-worn tyres as it takes on a mixed load.

Right: Joseph Eva Ltd was an old established private company dating back to 1917. When operator licensing was introduced the fleet totalled about 70 vehicles plus 60 horses, and the business was described as being 'carmen, carriers, haulage contractors and wharfingers'. A 1939 listing quotes the fleet as 100 vans plus the 60 horses, with depots at two locations in London, plus two wharves in Bermondsey. This 1934 model BB Ford tilt van was typical of the fleet, when the BTC take-over came in April 1949, and did not last long in BRS operation. Originally listed as Unit A80, Eva's later became 42A Shoreditch group.

Seen unloading Redpath Brown steel roof sections for the 1951 Festival of Britain Concert Hall, is an ERF eightwheeler and dolly type trailer which was originally part of the P.A. Carter fleet. A heavily braced front bolster has been added to keep the load off the cab, and a temporary turntable fitted over the rear bogie of the vehicle. As No.78 in the Carter fleet, the vehicle later became 5A116 with Blackwall Tunnel group.

Above: G.V. Dennis established his transport business in Nottingham in 1928, becoming a limited company as Robin Hood Transport Ltd in 1941. Sherwood Transport Ltd was taken over in July 1944 and Dove & Dove Ltd acquired in June 1946. A reflection of the expansion is provided by the fact that the claimed unladen tonnage in 1939 was 50 tons, this rising to no less than 240 tons in 1949 at the time of nationalisation. There were 30 units on A-licence, five on A-contract, 15 B-licences and two on C-licence as service vehicles. Main traffic flows were to Liverpool, London, Glasgow, Manchester and the Eastern counties.

Left: The old chain-drive Scammells were a legend in their time, and the rigid six was a part of that. The shaft drive model was introduced at the 1933 Commercial Motor Show, and this too became popular with transport operators, much publicity being given to companies which took several of them into their fleets such as C.D. & T., General Roadways, Fisher Renwick and R. Keetch. One of the vehicles from the Keetch fleet is shown as it appeared soon after the BRS take-over early in 1949.

Left: Longton Transport Ltd of King Street, Fenton, Stoke-on-Trent was incorporated in February 1929, and within ten years operating a fleet of 38 vehicles on A-licence. The company were keen on Thornycrofts operating a fleet of them in pre-war days, a practice which continued as this 1948 model shows. Under BRS the Longton depot formed the basis for 31E group.

Below: Fred Rose Ltd was established by Mr. Fred Rose in October 1927, and the business gradually expanded to provide services to London, the Midlands and the Northwest of the country. Traffic was mainly in linoleum, paper and foodstuffs, plus subcontract work for other hauliers. Branch offices were established at London, Liverpool and Wigan in order to secure better back loading to Lancashire. Most of the 24 vehicles taken over by BRS were second-hand, this 1939 Foden twinsteer coming into the Rose fleet in November 1941.

Left: S. Green & Sons Ltd of Erdington began operations in 1920, under the control of Mr. S. Green and his son H. Green. At the time of licensing by the West Midlands licensing authority, the fleet stood at 21 vehicles, and a report of 1939 quotes the fleet as being 22 six- and eight-wheelers of AEC manufacture. The company was acquired by BRS toward the end of 1948, allocated the reference Y1, later becoming Unit E8: S. Green & Sons (BTC) Ltd. The photograph shows an AEC eightwheeler - rebuilt from an earlier machine - alongside what appears to be a second-hand sixwheeler (GW2100), both vehicles having the BRS emblem slapped on the cab quarter panel. Greens operated many 'rebuilt' AECs in their fleet.

Below: One of the many Albions in the Sutton & Co. fleet, this 1947 model CX3 is seen parked close to the Manchester depot in Radium Street, just off the Oldham Road. Sutton & Co. operated from two main bases in London and in Manchester, and the company consisted of two separate operating companies reflecting the differing locations. There were about 20 branches located around the country, including Belfast and Dublin at one time.

Right: The origins of W.H. Bowker go back to just after the Great War, when William Bowker set up business at Blackburn, Lancs. By the mid 1930s there were 14 vehicles operating from Craig Street, while at the outbreak of war a move had been made to Stansfield Street Garage and there were 26 vehicles on A-licence. Upon acquisition in July 1949, the vehicles listed totalled 47 actually licensed, plus two others and a number of trailers. This 1946 Atkinson-Dyson articulated low-loader weighed 9ton l4cwt in licensing trim, it being originally No. 136 in Bowker days but renumbered 24C81 in the BRS fleet.

Above: Unit C174, Stansfield Street Garage, Blackburn, first appeared in the RHE Gazetteer in September 1949, for this was the address of W.H. Bowker Ltd, a staunch opposer of nationalisation. This photograph shows one of Bowker's 14B Leyland 'Beaver' trailer outfits parked in the area close to Tooley Street, SE1 in April 1950, by which time the BRS headboard had been attached.

Left: Another of W.H. Bowker's vehicles showing the gradual transformation to BRS identity. Old No.10 has had its dark blue livery marred by the red and white headboard, the hungry lion on the cab door, and the allocated fleet number of 24C73. It is pictured in the late afternoon sun, sheeted and roped ready for the night trunk driver to emerge from the 'digs' nearby.

Right: A fine September day in 1949 sees this tidy little Karrier 'Bantam' artic of Unit B17 West George Street, Glasgow parked outside the British Railways travel office in Dundee. The four wheel 'Bantam' tractors were used by some operators in preference to the Scammell MH because of their greater stability, and the wide-spaced landing gear of the trailer also provided a better footing when being loaded uncoupled. No.304 in the Wordie fleet looks quite smart with its polished radiator grille, much superior to the painted surrounds usually fitted. The folding cranking handle is a nice touch, as is the solitary headlight, but why should the unit sport no less than five identity discs in the windscreen?

Below: The Warpool Transport Company first started its Lancashire-London trunk runs in 1924, building up a fleet of over 20 vehicles which were based in the Liverpool and Warrington area, but maintaining a London base. This 1934 AEC eightwheeler was obtained second-hand, and shows signs of being re-engined with a somewhat longer diesel! Upon passing into BRS hands, the Warpool base at Sutton Street, Warrington became part of 5C Warrington group. Photographed in Holloway in 1950, the low brick building in the background is a reminder of wartime days when it served as an air-raid shelter.

Left: The seemingly endless girders of the Liverpool Overhead Railway acted as a steel spine to Liverpool's docks, and many people have expressed their sorrow that they were not saved. Here they stand near Pierhead, watched over by the tower of St. Nicholas's church, as one of W.B. Bell & Sons' Leyland 'Beaver' tippers waits in the weak sunshine of a July day in 1949. The A- and B-licenced fleet of 50 was controlled by the partners. Binning and Stanley Bell from premises at Berse, Wrexham.

Below: London Scottish Transport Ltd was fortunate in one way, for the name was perpetuated by BRS as it named 63B group 'London Scottish'. The company was incorporated in April 1938 with a base at Falkirk Road, Larbert, Stirlingshire; later a move was made to Clyde Street and Armour Street, Glasgow. The BTC acquired the company during 1949, allocating the reference Unit B120, later to become 63B group. The Maudslay was registered in Motherwell & Wishaw in 1949, this being one of the Scottish licensing authorities slowly working its way through the two letter registrations. The first number was issued in 1920; it took another 30 years just to get halfway to 9999!

Below: With the sheet neatly folded, a Scammell R8 from the fleet of All British Carriers Ltd, waits for instructions before reversing into the unloading bay. The vehicle has travelled up from South Wales overnight, with a load of sheet steel for an office furniture company. It carries no identification save the old fleet number 255, there being no group name or Unit number displayed. This was not unusual for this period, August 1950, when many companies were continuing to function almost as before, often with the same managers as in the days of private ownership. The location is Westminster, and the Pikes O-type is turning left into Ebury Bridge Road.

Above: An index of registration marks indicates this vehicle, CN9655, was the last to be registered in Gateshead in 1940. With an address listed as Baltic Chambers, Quayside, Newcastle-on-Tyne, it is perhaps fitting that this long wheelbase ERF should be photographed on the quayside just after G. Gowland Ltd passed into BRS ownership in late 1949. Under BRS Unit No.D77 Gowland was linked with Joseph M. Prior, J. Baxter and Joseph Reach, who were presumably associate companies, the operating address later being known as just Quayside, Newcastle group 7D, but by 1953 this had been absorbed into Newcastle group.

Above: William Wisely & Sons Ltd was one of the swath of Scottish transport companies acquired by the BTC soon after being established. The Aberdeen-based operator had its beginnings in the pre motor era in 1908, and by the late 1930s a total of over 60 vehicles were being operated. The business controlled from Virgina Street, Aberdeen became Unit B16 under BRS ownership, it later being absorbed into 1B Aberdeen General group, which mostly handled the dock and local traffic of the area.

Left: At first sight this looks like one of the original Bouts-Tillotson vehicles, for it bears the Unit No. A3 and the Bouts-Tillotson name and style of fleet number. But in fact the vehicles was first registered in February 1950, whereas Bouts-Tillotson was one of the original large groups to be acquired by the BTC in 1948, being listed in the first edition of the RTE Monthly List of Acquired Undertakings.

For many haulage companies operating in pre-nationalisation days, the four wheel vehicle with drawbar trailer was a much better proposition than the big rigid eightwheelers or maximum capacity artics of the period. The 'wagon and drag' concept provided the flexibility so often needed in mixed traffic work, which could be varied by seasonal or other outside influences. One drawback was the need for two men on this layout of vehicle, but this was not too much of a problem with wages so low. Still sporting the name of its previous owner, this 1935 'Beaver', which was one of ten similar chassis taken over, looks decided weary. The driver's door has a definite sag to it, and the rear springs so weak that there is hardly room to put a hand between tyre and mudguard!

Left: Pictured crossing London Bridge in 1951, is an L1586 model Atkinson operated by Battersea group (25A), which was based on the premises of J.R. Munday Ltd in Battersea Bridge Road, which still existed in 1998. The load appears to be boxes of oranges, which could have originated from a ship or riverside warehouse along the Thames, and with the prospect of a fine day the driver has dispensed with the sheets.

Right: This Scammell photograph shows the swansong of General Roadways in the shape of a vehicle ordered by Transport Services, but delivered to General Roadways (BTC) Ltd. It is finished in the all-over red of BRS, complete with headboard and lions and wheels on the doors, yet still with the old style fleet number within the T.S star design. Sometime later the vehicle became 43A85.

Right: Resplendent in its new livery, a 1949 Scammell 'Scarab' of the Bouts-Tillotson Transport (BTC) Ltd fleet is posed to show the lettering layout adopted for vehicles of voluntarily acquired companies. As Bouts-Tillotson was acquired during 1948, it is doubtful if this vehicle ever appeared in the red and cream colours of the old company. At this stage the old company fleet number series was still in use, the 33A group numbers would appear later. Location of the photograph is the yard in front of the depot in Waterden Road E15.

Right: This rather weary looking Albion dates from 1937 and is shown in its first coat of BRS red, with the style of lettering layout adopted by many units soon after acquisition. The body dropsides bear the legend 'Robinson's Transport (Beccles) Ltd' which was the name of the original owner, and there is no Unit number or other form of identification, save for the usual British Road Services and the hungry lion on the door. The vehicle was photographed in June 1949, and the location is on the approach to St. Katherine's Way with the Tower of London just visible in the background.

Above: Soon after the formation of BRS, the press were invited to the BTC headquarters at Marylebone and treated to a display of vehicles prepared in the new livery. One of the vehicles in that display was this Maudslay 'Meritor', which represented the type of long distance haulage vehicle envisaged for the new services. The vehicle was FAY8, a vehicle delivered in September 1948 to what was now Kinders Transport (BTC) Ltd, and the photograph shows it in the mid-day sunshine parked alongside Marylebone station. In their hurry to get the vehicle ready for display, the paintshop applied the wrong 'lion-and-wheel' transfer to the cab door - it's facing backwards! Interestingly, all the Maudslay eightwheelers supplied to BRS were built to 'Spec 27', which called for a special hydraulic accumulator, charged by a drive from the gearbox, which supplied power for the brakes at low speeds.

Right: A rather weary looking 'Hippo' of Blythe & Berwick seen near Tower Bridge in April 1950, by which time it had received a coat of red paint and some BRS lettering, yet retained the original fleet number and a depot telephone number. Upon nationalisation the Blythe & Berwick fleet contained 37 vehicles and seven trailers. Although predominantly Leyland which embraced SQ2, 'Bull', 'Leviathan', 'Buffalo', 'Terrier', 'Hippo', 'Cub' and 'Steer' models, there were also AEC, Albion, Commer, ERF and Foden - a real mixture!

Left: Pictured standing outside the Burnley premises of Oswald Tillotson Ltd, is this impressive Maudslay 'Meritor' freshly painted in BRS green, and lettered for Unit D28 Leeds. The bodybuilders, Oswald Tillotson Ltd, had acquired the old haulage company Bouts Brothers in 1933, only to find themselves acquired by Holdsworth & Hanson Ltd in 1935. BRS Unit D28 was the designation given to the Holdsworth & Hanson operation based at Wortley Low Mills, Whitehall Road, Leeds, and the old Bouts-Tillotson depot at Jack Lane, Leeds came under the London base of that company, and were initially included in Unit A3.

Above: Kinders Garage & Haulage Ltd was based at Blaby, Leicestershire being established in 1922. The company passed into the Transport Services group sometime during the 1940s, but remained under the capable management of Miss Alice M. Walker, who became a legend of her time. This photograph shows one of the ex Kinder's Leyland rigid eight dropsides, which was typical of the fleet and is shown in laden condition in 1950. The early style of BRS lettering is apparent with the old company name displayed as well as the original fleet number within the TS group star.

Right: As the acquisitions progressed, BRS found itself inheriting many outstanding contracts for the supply of new vehicles. The fledgling national carrier needed a constant flow of new chassis to replace many of those that were at the end of their useful life, but in some instance new vehicles were being delivered which did not conform to the planned standards of the BRS fleet. This Scammell was an early delivery, showing the livery adopted as the new organisation moved away from the Unit system, into the planned grouping arrangement. The semi-lowloading trailer was used mainly for the transport of reels of electrical cable from manufacturers in the Thames-side area to customers nation-wide.

Left: Among the thousands of vehicles acquired by BRS, there were a few of the lesser known makes such as this 1948 Proctor in service with Unit D175 Fred Cook, Hull. Fred Cook first started transport services in May 1930, became a private limited company in May 1932 and was acquired by the BTC in the summer of 1949. The vehicle is seen parked near the old Fred Cook (Transport) Ltd London depot in Druid Street, SE1 in 1950.

Below: Three ex Fisher Renwick Scammells -'Rook', 'Raven' and 'Plover', seen parked in Muswell Hill depot in March 1950, by which time they had received their first coat of BRS green. There was a variety of lettering for fleets in the early days of BRS, some of the ex Fisher Renwick vans were lettered 'British Road Services, London-Manchester' others 'Fisher Renwick (BTC) Ltd, British Road Services' or 'Unit C33 Fisher Renwick Manchester, British Road Services'. The Muswell Hill depot in Coppetts Road, was specifically designed as a major parcels handling facility, being strategically placed close to two major routes: the A406 North Circular Road, and the old Great North Road through Finchley. It continued in use throughout the life of BRS parcels operations.

Left: Soon after being acquired in the early part of 1949, BRS Unit B47 took delivery of this CX3L model Albion. The vehicle was unregistered when it was photographed for the suppliers, and the records show that it was designed to carry between 170 and 230 sheep in the detachable container. Weighing in at 6ton 12cwt unladen, it was identified as number 31 in the fleet originally owned by MacLennan who operated from Conon Bridge, which is situated at the head of Cromarty Firth near Inverness.

Right: Pictured on the northern approach to Tower Bridge, is this example of an Albion CX27 twinsteer insulated van in service with 5A Blackwall Tunnel. The cross-boarding of the bodywork provides the clue that the vehicle originally came from E. Wells & Son Ltd, a contractor with roots going back to the beginning of the century.

Below: A BRS advertising postcard, showing four of the Bedford articulated bulk grain carriers provided by 4A East Kent group, and advocating the savings in labour, time and sacks for traders with large quantities to move. Similar publicity was aimed at the bulk movements of raw sugar from factory to refinery, malt in bulk for breweries, and carbon black for tyres.

"EAST KENT GROUP" — BRITISH ROAD SERVICES
8-TON BULK GRAIN CARRIERS
We have the Vehicles.   Save Labour, Time and Sacks!
PHONE CANTERBURY 2258.

Right: As part of the BRS standard vehicle programme, a large number of Seddon four wheel rigids and tractor units were purchased from early in 1953. The pair of Mark 5L 7-tonners shown here were among those allocated to 6A Bermondsey at Silwood Street, the site being formerly the depot of Gammon & Dicker Ltd. Saturday was a good day for a visit, for the majority of the fleet was at rest with perhaps washing down and minor repairs being completed. Staff were usually helpful to young enthusiasts, and here one is busy noting new additions to the fleet since his previous visit.

Left: The AEC Mark III model 3871 chassis was very popular in many fleets around the country, and the very first was supplied to Pickfords in 1948. BRS inherited some in its early days, and then later ordered batches alongside the contemporary Leyland 'Octopus' chassis. The example shown was one of a series of 80 delivered early in 1953, it being allocated to 6A Bermondsey.

Above: This 1945 Seddon artic of Bermondsey group retains the austere look of the wartime days, with its very plain cab and almost featureless radiator. The semi-trailer is of interest, for it is fitted with a front bolster more akin to steel haulage than boxes of fruit. The scene is Spitalfields market on a Saturday afternoon, when most of the businesses have closed, and drivers are left to rope down loads before they return to base. Spitalfields market dates back to 1682, and after passing through several hands was acquired by the City of London Corporation in 1920. Most of the buildings date from the 1928 rebuilding programme.

Left: Although strides toward a standardised fleet were well on the way by the time the Transport Act 1953 was passed, there were still considerable numbers of non-standard vehicles within the ranks of BRS. This 1940 model ERF was still in regular work with 7A South East London General Services when photographed at Canning Town in May 1954.

Left: Among the various vehicle types which BRS adopted as 'standard', was the ERF in both solo and artic layout. This example, working from 7A Camberwell, was recently in service when photographed by Jim Wyndham as it crossed the northern approach to Tower Bridge. To modern eyes the absence of a second wiper and direction indicators seems rather parsimonious, but then we know that the trailer attendant doesn't need to see through a rain-spattered screen, and he can be relied upon to extend an arm just before the outfit turns left!

Right: Some load transhipping had just taken place on this Saturday morning, when the photographer framed the 1951 Maudslay-badged 'Mammoth Major' box van parked outside 9A Searles Road. It is believed that the vehicle was originally ordered by a haulier, and BRS had subsequently taken delivery and allocated it to Camberwell. It quickly passed to 9A Contracts as a spare for the Mackintosh contract, although it was used for other work. The short rear overhang to the body does suggest that it was intended for trailer work, but it was never seen in operation that way. Another mystery is that frail front bumper, which doesn't appear capable of protecting anything, nor is it sturdy enough to be used as an emergency towing bar.

Left: It is hard to believe that this was the scene alongside the A406 North Circular Road on a Wednesday morning in July 1953. But this section of road is still in use, being located between the southern end of the M1 and Brent Cross shopping centre, Hendon. The ERF tractor was one of the number produced for the civilian market during the war, at a time when the Ministry of War Transport was urging ERF to expand production to meet the shortfall of tractor units from Scammell. The outfit shown is a matching pair (25A576 and 25A577), and the semi-low loader with hand winch was useful for handling items such as the cable reels shown.

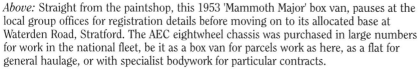

Above: Straight from the paintshop, this 1953 'Mammoth Major' box van, pauses at the local group offices for registration details before moving on to its allocated base at Waterden Road, Stratford. The AEC eightwheel chassis was purchased in large numbers for work in the national fleet, be it as a box van for parcels work as here, as a flat for general haulage, or with specialist bodywork for particular contracts.

Right: Two of the depot staff watch as the driver of this 34A Parcels Services AEC 'Matador' reverses into the depot after dropping off the trailer. The vehicle was one of a batch supplied to the Express Motor Bodyworks at Enfield in late 1948, for bodywork and then delivery to Carter, Paterson & Co. for parcels trunk work from Macclesfield Road. Carter, Paterson had long been users of lift vans or containers, such as shown here, but they could only be removed at the CP depots which had the equipment. With most CP depots not being rail connected there was little possibility of the containers being trunked by rail.

Right: Many of the long distance operations of BRS were handled by the lorry and trailer configuration before articulation was widely adopted. The trailer allowed for a certain degree of flexibility in meeting traffic demands, with it being dispensed with altogether in slack periods. But they did demand handling in depot confines, as well as being used for collection or deliveries as required. This 1947 ERF (ex Baker, Southampton) articulated unit was converted to a ballast tractor for use at the old Sutton & Co. parcels depot in Whitecross Street, EC1.

Left: Parcels Services Leyland 'Badger' showing its Sutton & Co. parentage by way of the own-build cab and bodywork, plus the old fleet number within the 34A group designation. The main London premises of Sutton & Co. was located in Whitecross Street, EC1 on the opposite side of the road to where this vehicle is parked.

Right: The three-section dropside body of this Maudslay-badged AEC eightwheeler, was very useful for containing a load of boxed shoes from the nearby warehouse of Lilley & Skinner Ltd. Based at Thurrock group, it was probably more used to agricultural use or for work in connection with a nearby cement works, but the reason for the very high sides is not known.

Below: Arms folded, the driver of this rigid sixwheel Scammell waits for help with unloading of the packing cases, destined for H.Comoy & Co. Ltd, who were located on the corner of Penton Street and Pentonville Road, N1. Originally delivered to Kneller & Chandler, the 1938 machine was at first allocated to BRS Bishopsgate Group passing to Blackwall Tunnel in 1951, but by 1953 when this photograph was taken it had been transferred to Islington (43A).

Right: While some of the larger BRS parcels' depots could boast huge loading banks with perhaps moving conveyors, in some corners of the empire a bombed site served as a tranship point from C&D van to night trunk vehicle. Here we see such an operation taking place at what was known as Pentonville Road depot, with an ex Bouts-Tillotson Scammell taking aboard packages collected by the Bedford OW in the background.

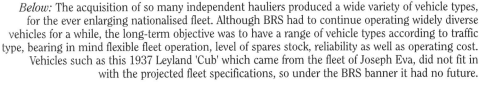

Below: The acquisition of so many independent hauliers produced a wide variety of vehicle types, for the ever enlarging nationalised fleet. Although BRS had to continue operating widely diverse vehicles for a while, the long-term objective was to have a range of vehicle types according to traffic type, bearing in mind flexible fleet operation, level of spares stock, reliability as well as operating cost. Vehicles such as this 1937 Leyland 'Cub' which came from the fleet of Joseph Eva, did not fit in with the projected fleet specifications, so under the BRS banner it had no future.

Left: Large capacity four wheel furniture vans were something of a rarity in the BRS general haulage fleet, the majority of this type of vehicle being operated by Pickfords in their Household Removal department. This Perkins-engined ET6 Ford was one of a number originally operated by BRS Tottenham group, later to form part of Pickfords' new Furniture Carriage Service which was set up to provide a fleet of large capacity vans for the furniture trade which in London, was centred on the Lee valley area, taking in Tottenham, Edmonton, Hackney and parts of London's east end.

This fine view of Covent Garden is dated December 1952 and shows the produce market from the south, with the usual melee of vehicles, porters and barrows. Careful scrutiny of the photograph reveals a selection of vehicles, BRS being represented by two Albions and an ERF from 22D North Leeds group, plus a possible QX Commer from the same area. There is also an unidentified 5-tonner from Stepney group, and a post-war Leyland in the far distance. There are several vehicles belonging to fruit and vegetable wholesalers, plus the universal British Railways Scammells with flat trailers and insulated containers. An O-type Bedford of Union Cartage is parked to the right, a vehicle more at home in Smithfield market than here.

Above: An organisation the size of BRS required adequate servicing and repair facilities at locations around the country. They inherited a wide range of servicing arrangements, varying from the man that did it all himself, to the large fleets with well-organised regular schedules, plus those operators who chose to use the services of local specialised dealers. One such BRS facility was the Silvertown Repair Centre located at Bradfield Road, E16. The building was taken over with Mack's Hauliers Ltd in June 1950, a company running a mixed fleet but with the emphasis on tankers. The AEC 'Matador' (EA36) shown, was a 1944 machine which came into BRS hands via Woolwich Transport (King & Sparrow) in 1950. It was later transferred to other BRS repair centres at Waterden Road and Ipswich before being sold.

Right: There had been few road haulage enthusiasts prior to the arrival of BRS, but the new large organisation provided an opportunity for students of lorry fleets to record a huge chunk of the then existing vehicles on the road. In due course most vehicles became easily identifiable, with fleet numbers and code letters which fell into a recognisable pattern. In the early days of BRS ownership, most vehicles retained the identification allotted by its previous owner, if the vehicles had ever carried any numbers. Some vehicles were repainted with the new Unit number which aided recognition, although not identifying each vehicle. The introduction of the depot and group system of numbering, brought a greater sense of order to the fleet, and enabled number recorders to start getting the vehicles into lists.

The local clock tower dominates this scene of the original Campbeltown depot, with an early post-war Albion livestock vehicle being prepared for work. Although only 60 miles from the Glasgow base of the group, Campbeltown was some nine hours journey by lorry, such is the geographical position of Kintyre. A new depot was built in 1958.

BRITISH ROAD SERVICES
ARGYLL BRANCH
CAMPBELTOWN DEPOT

BRITISH ROAD SERVICES

These four photographs of Silwood Street depot in Bermondsey illustrate four of the eightwheel vehicles which were part of the regular trunk runs to Scotland in 1953.

The old London Scottish Transport depot at Arch 453, Silwood Street, in Bermondsey, was alongside and under the railway as the address implies. Originally listed as Unit B120, with services to Glasgow, Edinburgh, Manchester, Liverpool, Dundee and Aberdeen, the depot was later allocated as 6A Bermondsey under the group scheme. This was one of the major London groups, for it included ten original operator's depots, all within a couple of miles to the southeast of London Bridge.

Silwood Street depot was reasonably accessible for the maximum capacity vehicles which made up a large proportion of its fleet, for it handled much of the trunk traffic to Scotland, the north, north-east and north-west regions. Naturally there was considerable traffic locally, for within its catchment area was a large number of industrial premises, plus Surrey Commercial Docks and the innumerable Thames-side wharves along the south side of the river.

Above: The Jensen lightweight six tonner was a popular machine during the 1940s and 1950s, for operators requiring bodywork for carrying long or bulky loads. Many furniture manufacturers and removal contractors found the high capacity vans ideal for their work, and BRS inherited quite a number of the vehicles from the latter. This 1947 model JNSN of 63B London Scottish group was one of many operating across the border, and is pictured negotiating the narrow streets of Baldock, Herts in 1951.

Left: The small artics which came into BRS hands from the old railway agents J. Nall and Wordie, were well suited to the general collection and delivery work among the docks, wharves and warehouses of Scottish cities. This late model Karrier 'Bantam' was lettered as 60B Douglas group in 1951, but was working in the Glasgow area delivering tobacco leaf in wooden containers. Unusually the vehicle is fitted with the Karrier BJ automatic coupling gear, which featured trailer landing gear with wheels outside those on the tractor, demanding a narrow track.

Below: Although not as high as the box vans used by operators such as Fisher Renwick or Bouts-Tillotson, this DG model Foden was an asset to group 9C Liverpool Parcels. The mixed loads they carried demanded a large volume van, even if the maximum weight capacity was not attained. An impressive vehicle by any standards, this 1946 machine basks in the lunchtime sunshine sharing the road with a pair of Austin cars, while a handful of coaches park on a bomb-site near to Kings Cross.

Top: An exhibit at the Royal Highland Show of 1952, was this Albion HD57 eightwheel flat with triple deck livestock container, having a stated capacity of 150 sheep or 12 fat cattle! Fresh in its coat of red with tyres suitably blackened, it carries fleet number 44B306 of East Lothian & Borders, being based at Haddington, East Lothian.

Above: London Scottish Transport Ltd ordered a number of AEC 3451 model chassis in the late 1940s, and had started to take delivery when nationalisation came along. This example, GM4990, was the last of the batch, being delivered to BRS Unit B120 in April 1950. An unusual feature of the vehicles was that sliding doors were specified, and as can be seen, the little opening window section was repeated on both sides of the cab.

Above: The day shunter finishes off the sheeting and roping of 24C138 of West Blackburn group, which is parked in Hilldrop Crescent, Holloway in June 1950, and just discernible on the vehicle sheet is 'W.H. Bowker Unit C174 Blackburn'. The extreme set-forward of the cab on the Albion CX7 twin-steer is immediately apparent, showing the layout of two axles for the load and one for the engine and cab.

Right: A fine example of the FG 6/15 model Foden eightwheeler, which BRS acquired in considerable numbers in the 1950s. This example was photographed in June 1951 when just about a year old, and is seen unloading quality printing paper to one of the print houses in the Stamford Street, SE1 area. Many of the Fodens acquired by BRS were allocated to the north-west of England, for the marque was very popular with transport contractors in that part of the country; this vehicle was in service with 69C Bolton & Bury group.

Left: The Scammell articulated eightwheeler had been the mainstay of many long distance haulage operations, the modern vehicles replacing those of earlier years. Not so widespread was the use of large box vans on similar chassis, such as the 1953 version shown here in service with 64C Greenheys. The Scammell traditions of single tyres all round, as well as the radiused trailer front, are highlighted in this shot of 64C544 parked near the cafe in Holloway Road.

Below: In the early days of its existence, BRS frequently took a display stand at the agricultural shows around the country. In 1951 this Bedford S-type of 20D York group, was used to publicise the facility available to farmers and stockbreeders for the transport of farm animals.

Above: North Hull group included the fleet of the former operator Fred Cook (Transport) Ltd, a haulage company which began operations in May 1930, becoming a limited company two years later. Within a short while the fleet had grown to 30 vehicles. This photograph shows one of the AEC box vans which were engaged on regular runs between Hull and London, and is pictured in Buckingham Palace Road, with the old Imperial Airways (later BOAC) terminal in the background. The vehicle was rated as a 15-tonner, and had an unladen weight of 7ton 16cwt when it entered service in June 1947.

These four photographs are grouped together because they show a continuous section of Seward Street EC1, which included the London depot of Holdsworth & Hanson Ltd, plus an entrance to the headquarters site of Carter, Paterson & Co. which contained a BRS repair facility. For anyone interested, the majority of the buildings shown in the photographs were still standing late in 1997. Only the facade of The Rest House remains, the old CP stables are a car park, the repair depot is a metal warehouse and the parcels depot was a builders' merchants although plans were afoot to demolish it to make way for flats. The old Taylor, Walker & Co. public house 'The Leopard', in the background of the fourth view, still exists, although refurbished.

Below: The first view shows the beginning of Seward Street taken from the Goswell Road end, with a typical Holdsworth & Hanson AEC Mammoth Major box van parked outside The Rest House cafe, which was situated on the corner of Mount Mills, an ancient Great Plague burial ground. Features of these vans were the open roof section for overhead loading, which was normally covered by a sheet when travelling; access to which was gained by the five hinged steps at the nearside front of the body, with a solitary grab handle at the roof edge.

Right: The Atkinson sixwheeler is seen parked just a few yards further along the road outside what used to be Carter, Paterson & Co's horse stabling. The shunt driver stands, arms akimbo, waiting for the photographer to get his shot, before completing the task of sheeting and roping.

Above: The third photograph shows a South Bradford group Maudslay 'Meritor', loaded with some secure metal containers for the safe transit of print. At this time it was numbered 43D55, but it later became P50D793 with a reorganisation of the parcels operation in that part of Yorkshire. The vehicle is parked alongside what was then a BRS repair centre, and the Seward Street parcels depot can be seen in the background with the rear end of a Bedford ballast tractor just visible.

Right: Reversed in on full lock, another of the impressive open-top vans has just managed to squeeze on to the run-in of the old Holdsworth & Hanson depot, with the rolling shutter pulled down for security. This was one of the original H&H trunk vehicles operating from Huddersfield (42D).

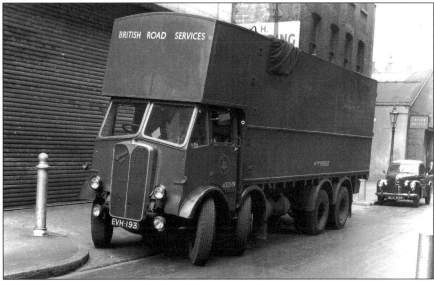

Above: A quiet scene in Baldock, Herts in June 1951 with a Maudslay 'Mogul' drawbar outfit of 43D South Bradford group, making the turn on the old A1 trunk road going north. Bradford was well covered by transport companies in the days prior to BRS, so the area became home to three BRS groups: Central Bradford 44D, South Bradford 43D and West Bradford 47D.

Right: An example of the high capacity box vans turned out by Oswald Tillotson, for what had been the parent company Holdsworth & Hanson Ltd. This late 1949 Maudslay was allocated to South Bradford (43D), which took in the past operations of Burrill, Crow, Bells and Holdsworth & Burrill.

Below: Another workhorse of the old Holdsworth & Hanson fleet was this Albion CX5 sixwheeler, which often worked with a drawbar trailer. It is seen in Goswell Road, close to the London depot of its former owners, awaiting further instructions. Like its larger eightwheel counterparts, the van is of the characteristic open-top variety, with a hefty front lowing hitch for trailer shunting, which can be swung out of the way for hand cranking. Also worthy of note is another classic, a 1932 Armstrong-Siddeley saloon parked in the distance.

Right: If anything epitomises the old style of long distance parcels carrying, then it must be the classic maximum capacity vans such as this 1936 AEC Mark II 'Mammoth Major'. An ex Holdsworth & Hanson vehicle based at 43D South Bradford group, it was nearing the end of its operational life when photographed in May 1952, but it still retains the features of a well designed outfit.

Below: A freshly painted AEC 'Monarch' destined for 4E Cheapside Birmingham group stands outside the BRS bodyshops in Water Street, Manchester. This could almost be described as the 'standard' lorry body of the period, being a double-dropside type with cab height headboard and a drop tailboard. Constructed mainly of timber with steel fittings, the body features detachable side centre pillars for easy conversion to a flat. The cab is of single skin metal panelling on an ash frame, with two bucket type seats finished in brown leathercloth. The right-hand panel of the two-piece windscreen is of the hinged pattern, and protective metal bars are fitted to the cab rear window. Simple steps and grab handles on either side of the cab provide ease of entry, and separate steps on the front panel enable the driver to reach radiator filler cap and windscreen.

Left: After delivering the load of steel sections in nearby Wisbech, the driver of this Atkinson decides to pause at Mr. Cousins' stall alongside the A47 to get the wife a punnet of strawberries, before heading back to Sheffield. After a few years in BRS hands, many vehicles took on this bland appearance with a well flatted coat of red, and no indication of its group, base or service. The 63D Park group was centred on the fleets of Gregorys Transport, Bramall, and Griffiths Transport.

Overleaf: A view of Cheapside, Birmingham depot loading bank with three locally-based vehicles present. The Leyland 'Octopus' carries a sizeable headboard which announces the 'British Road Services Birmingham London Nightly Express Service', the destinations of which can be changed as necessary.

Below: This beautifully turned out L1586 Atkinson was just a couple of months old, when photographed late in 1953. Allocated to 2E Coventry, it represented a large batch of Atkinsons purchased by BRS during the period of consolidation. Both rigid eightwheelers and fourwheel tractor units were put on the road, most of them in the north of England.

Left: An early morning scene outside the Dingley Road entrance to the BRS parcels depot at Macclesfield Road, which was the London centre of the old Carter, Paterson & Co's parcel business. The Scammell has journeyed down from Birmingham and the ropes are in the process of being removed. This vehicle was originally No.410 in the Eastern Roadways fleet, being purchased in June 1947 at a cost of £3640.

Below: The area around Tower Hill and Royal Mint Street used to be very busy with lorry traffic, for it led to the last bridge crossing of the Thames, as well as providing a useful parking space. St. Katherine's and London docks were close by, as well as numerous riverside wharves and warehouses around the Pool of London. In this photograph a pair of Atkinson flats from 61E South Nottingham, pause while one of the drivers telephones for further instructions. An Albion box van of 50A Muswell Hill group is seen passing in the background, while a van for The Star newspaper based on the Austin taxicab chassis, exits speedily left along East Smithfield.

Above and left: The major parcels depot in London was the Macclesfield Road premises of Carter, Paterson & Co. which was located in a triangle bounded by Macclesfield Road, City Road and Dingley Road. The site was at the southern end of City Road Basin, a short branch of the Regents Canal, and was previously used by Pickfords in the 19th century as the London City dock for their canal barge operations. Later this part of the City Basin was filled in to make way for a depot handling road vehicles, then in the 1930s an impressive parcels handling depot was constructed to replace the old CP premises in nearby Goswell Road. The two photographs here show a pair of vehicles from 60E Nottingham Parcels, waiting at the Dingley Road entrance of the depot to be called in to unload. It is interesting to note that both vehicles carry advertising posters, for this was common practice going back several decades. While the Leyland carries a poster for Cherry Blossom boot polish, and the Maudslay one for Mackeson stout, note that the trailer of the Leyland displays one of the BRS posters, which in this instance depicts an S-type Bedford articulated van.

Left: At locations remote from BRS premises where there was a large throughput of traffic, it was found expedient to provide on-site office facilities by the use of mobile offices. This old Morris-Commercial box van was converted in BRS workshops to form a traffic office for documentation at the large Morris car plant at Oxford. Similar on-site offices were provided at docks in London and Liverpool.

Below: The British Transport Commission acquired a considerable number of Vulcans in both four wheel rigid and artic tractor form, some dating from pre-war days, plus others purchased by private hauliers in post-war days when new vehicles were at a premium. A number of the last models in production were to be seen in BRS colours, the one illustrated being registered as late as 1953. This artic from 62F Medway group is seen outside a Thames-side printing works with a load of newsprint which probably originated from the Bowater plant located on the River Medway in Kent.

Above: The forward control Commer QX 7-tonner with its underfloor engine, was quite popular with haulage contractors and C-licence operators alike. This example was photographed at work carrying the remains of a railway bridge on the Isle of Wight, and interestingly the small mobile crane used for loading was also part of the local BRS 26F group. The lorry bodywork has been modified with a front bolster to keep the long steel sections off the cab, but with no such provision at the rear end, old wooden sleepers have been positioned to protect the tailboard.

Below: Much of the traffic to the Isle of Wight was controlled by the railways, either directly or through their cartage agents such as Chaplins, who were controlled by Pickfords, which in turn was owned by the mainline railway companies from 1933. This early 1939 Bedford WTL model is lettered as a 26F group vehicle, but was originally Pickfords M3458 for Chaplins. It was photographed in Ventnor in August 1952 performing local delivery work with a British Railways container.

Right: One aspect of haulage that has disappeared from our roads, is that of milk collection in individual churns. For very many years this was an everyday occurrence, with lorries plying the byways and lanes of the grazing areas, picking up the full churns from farms or roadside pick-up points, and leaving a number of empties for the next day. BRS took over this business from very many of the country hauliers, who carried out the service on behalf of the dairies and creameries which processed the milk, ready for bottling or onward transit in bulk to city centres.

Above: After a long period of planning and design, the first type of 'in house' vehicle for the nationalised fleet made its appearance in August 1952. Produced by Bristol Commercial Vehicles at their Brislington, Bristol works, the eight wheel chassis was a completely new venture for a company more used to building bus chassis. Designed for the maximum gross weight of 22tons for the period, the chassis featured a Leyland 9.8 litre six-cylinder engine with a Bristol clutch and five-speed constant mesh gearbox. It had a single driving axle with spiral bevel drive, plus further reduction by way of double helical gearing. The Westinghouse air brakes operated on the first, third and fourth axles, and on 36"x8" tyres all round the complete vehicle weighed about 7½tons complete with a platform body 24'-7" long.

Left: The Star Bodies facility at Star Works, Water Street, Manchester was reconstituted as Star Bodies (BTC) Ltd in 1948, and continued as a bodybuilding works for the RHE. This AEC Mammoth Major box van was an early production for parcels services, and was allocated to Central Bristol group. Later the bodyshops were transferred to a new location at Hollinwood Street, Manchester.

Above: The BRS group serving the northern part of Devon and part of Somerset was 5F, entitled Taunton and North Devon. It covered an area from Highbridge in the north, down to Bude, along the coast and then inland in a wide arc taking in Exeter, Wellington, Taunton and Bridgwater. The group was based at the High Street premises of the pre-nationalisation operator D.G. Bowerman, who continued on in BRS days as group manager. The group originally had 11 depots and the traffic included eggs and milk, potatoes and cattle, feeding stuffs and fertilisers through to agricultural machinery, plus of course a wide variety of industrial products and packaged foodstuffs. This impressive CX7 model Albion was photographed after loading 15 tons of animal feed at Wiveliscombe in Somerset.

Left: One facet of BRS operations that is not widely known was that it acquired a lime spreading business as part of one West Country haulier. The first photograph shows a short wheelbase Bedford O-type tipper loaded with bagged lime, and the lime is being emptied into the hopper type body of the spreader vehicle. The two drivers have chosen a sheltered position to carry out this hazardous task, and this 1952 photograph shows the complete absence of any protective equipment for the operation.

Above: In this second photograph the Bedford QL 4x4 spreader is busy at work, with a huge cloud of dust marking its progress across the field at a farm near Wheddon Cross, Somerset. The vehicle was based at Appledore in the Taunton and North Devon Group (5F).

Left: The ubiquitous Bedford O-type really lived up to its maker's slogan of "You See Them Everywhere", for they formed the basis for very many fleets up and down the country. The 5-ton dropside was the workhorse of countless small operators, and BRS must have acquired hundreds. This 1956 example is pictured in rural surroundings loading boxes of eggs at an egg packing station at Wiveliscombe, Somerset.

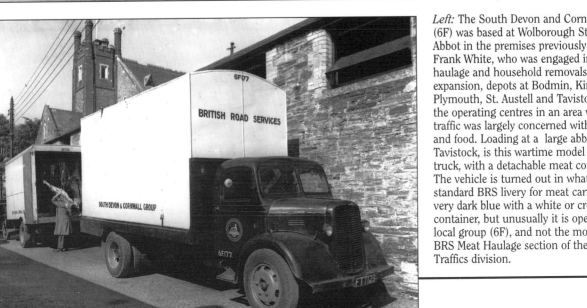

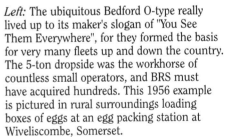

Left: The South Devon and Cornwall Group (6F) was based at Wolborough Street, Newton Abbot in the premises previously occupied by Frank White, who was engaged in general haulage and household removals. With expansion, depots at Bodmin, Kingsbridge, Plymouth, St. Austell and Tavistock made up the operating centres in an area where the traffic was largely concerned with agriculture and food. Loading at a large abbatoir in Tavistock, is this wartime model Dodge flat truck, with a detachable meat container. The vehicle is turned out in what was the standard BRS livery for meat cartage, namely very dark blue with a white or cream container, but unusually it is operated by the local group (6F), and not the more common BRS Meat Haulage section of the Special Traffics division.

Right: A fact not often appreciated, is the close connections that BRS had with farming communities, operating outside the main centres of population. Many small hauliers had grown up with close collaboration between local farmers, or the transport operation had grown out of farming. So the new organisation had to continue servicing such diverse traffics as animal feeds, farm produce, eggs, livestock, seeds and grain, but on a much grander scale. Seen loading cattle at a farm at Tavistock, is this large articulated transporter, helped by four men to control the animals in the lane. The trailer is lettered South Devon and Cornwall group (6F), but the Bedford OSS tractor is numbered in Pickfords fleet system and not BRS, and was used with other trailers as required. Numbered M5977 it was probably part of the old Chaplins railway cartage fleet, it later became 27F67, was based at Plymouth and painted green. After serving with BRS until 1953, it was then sold to British Railways.

Below: Group 28F Exeter Parcels was based on the old Carter, Paterson & Co. depot at Church Road, St. Thomas. This M-type Bedford 3-tonner is pictured at the loading bank, which is piled high with a typical assortment of packages included in the description of 'smalls'. Worthy of note is the large poster of a BRS eightwheeler on the van side; this was one of a series of full-colour pictures used to publicise the varying services of BRS in the early days of operation.

Right: Most BRS vehicles were provided with a low nameboard for the cab roof which carried the services name, but in some instances trunk vehicles were equipped with something more pronounced, as shown here. Seen alongside another vehicle in Hayes depot (48A) which was originally the home of H. Burgoine Ltd, is one of the Leyland rigid eights of 1G Newport group which regularly ran between south Wales and the London area. Often steel was transported up from the South Wales steelworks, and market produce or foodstuffs taken back.

Left: The weak sunshine of an April afternoon provides pleasant lighting conditions, for this photograph of this Swansea-based 'Mammoth Major', as it waits for sheets to be positioned and ropes secured over the load of vegetables. The vehicles from South Wales were often staged at High Wycombe, where the shunt or day drivers would take them on to their final destinations, often loaded with steel products. In this instance a return load of agricultural produce has been secured from Spitalfields market, and it will probably be back in Wales before dawn tomorrow.

Right: Still unregistered, a new Thornycroft PF/NR6 model 'Trusty', poses for its first photograph in the yard of the Basingstoke works. This example, with triple dropside bodywork, was lettered for No. 2G Wellington Group, Newport depot, which probably means that it was destined for Elliotts Transport depot in Alexandra Road, Newport or the Dock Street depot which provided trunk services to London and Liverpool.

Above: During 1951 a batch of AEC eightwheel chassis was acquired for Bury St. Edmunds group to service the large sugar beet factory of the British Sugar Corporation. As can be seen from the photograph, the vehicles were equipped with gable-roofed stout wooden bodywork for the transport of sugar in bulk, being loaded from above. Some of the sugar was delivered direct to customers for food use, whilst some went to other processors for further refining or conversion.

Right: It is Saturday lunchtime, and as local industry closes down for the weekend, the driver of Norwich group 1H11 has joined other drivers in a place of refreshment, before returning home. This vehicle, VG8394 was originally No. 82 in the Eastern Roadways fleet, being a 1936 14-tonner based at Bishops Stortford. In 1949 Norwich (1H), brought together the local operations of Eastern Roadways Ltd, H.G. Cushion Ltd, Giles & Bullen Ltd, E.R. Ives Ltd, PX (Eastern) Ltd, Bouts-Tillotson Ltd, Platts Bros and Direct Transport Services. These latter were to form Norfolk & Suffolk Parcels Group and never received IH fleet numbers.

Left: We can only speculate as to what the mate is saying to the driver, as he spots the photographer carefully framing this rather worn looking ERF. Originally supplied to Eastern Roadways in March 1938, old No. 124 tipped the scales at 7tons unladen, being equipped with lightweight cab and bodywork by Duramin. Original price for the vehicle was £3007, but upon nationalisation its value was set at just £323.

Right: The British Sugar Corporation was set up to handle the production of home-produced sugar extracted from sugarbeet. With plants at strategic locations around the country, the sugarbeet was brought in by both local farmers and hauliers. Naturally BRS gradually moved into this sphere of operation, as well as the handling of the raw sugar for onward transport for further refining or direct to other customers. Pictured at the large Bury St. Edmunds facility of BSC, this 1949 Vulcan o Peterborough group with a heavy wooden body, is being loaded with raw sugar via an overhead shute. Note that no roof doors are fitted to the body, a closely woven sheet will envelop the whole body after loading.

Above: Being positioned close to major brickworks at Peterborough and Whittlesey, BRS group 21H was responsible for handling large quantities of the building materials during the busy post-war housing boom. This ERF was originally operated by C.J. Tribe of Wisbech, being a DI641 model delivered in October 1945. This AEC-engined 13'11" wheelbase chassis carried an 18ft body and was factory-fitted with the swing-out front towing jaw for access to the cranking handle.

Right: With its closely spaced uprights and boarded tilt top, the bodywork of this AEC of Fordham group identifies the previous owner as having been H.A. Newport. However, Newport was acquired in November 1948, and this vehicle dates from early in 1950, so it was a case of BRS honouring the contract placed by the private haulier before they were nationalised. Actually this was no bad thing, because there was still a waiting list for vehicles of this quality, and the order was for four chassis which became HVE491-4. Signs of the times are the small estate of 'prefabs' to the left, and the fact that the vehicle was restricted to 20mph!

A pair of 1946 Dennis 'Max' 7-tonners pause outside The Plough near Biggleswade, Bedfordshire in July 1953. Both vehicles are from 23H Cambridge group, and are probably running back empty after delivering their load of local farm produce to market.

Contract Hire

The business of vehicles on contract hire is almost as old as the carrying industry itself, for even in the 19th century there were many cartage contractors willing to supply horsedrawn vans and even handcarts or box trikes on a regular basis to customers, often being painted in the individual livery.

For many carters the contract hire service was just a part of their everyday business, but to some it was far more attractive than running vans in competition with all the others in the carrying world, and they set out to specialise in the service.

But the sphere of contract hire is not without its aspirers, and fierce competition could be generated when a particularly lucrative contract came up for renewal. Obviously the larger customers demanding many vans were targeted by aggressive contractors, but some of the smaller contracts could be worthwhile, particularly if the vans were not going to be worked too hard.

In horsedrawn days the contractor usually supplied the horse, van and driver, with perhaps the customer supplying loading staff who knew the products. In later years the customer sometimes supplied his own driver, a feature which caused problems with vehicle licensing, the operating licence being issued to the person who employed the driver. So we find that after the A, B and C licences were issued, a contract vehicle might be operated under an A-contract licence if the driver was supplied by the haulage contractor, but a C-hiring licence was required if the customer supplied his own driver.

So BRS also came into the world of contract hire, and it began right at the beginning with the first flush of acquisitions in 1948. Transport Services Ltd, H & G Dutfield, Holdsworth & Hanson, and of course Hay's Wharf with Pickfords, Carter Paterson and Bean's were all into contract hire at various levels. Thomas Tilling, NMU, Charles Wells, R.J. Weeks, Fairclough, McNamara, Foulkes & Bailey and a host of others operated fleets of vehicles turned out in the colours of their customers, with the larger units holding a number of plain vans to cover servicing requirements.

Many of the contract vehicles were not only turned out in specific customer liveries, but often they were vehicles specifically bought for a particular contract. One customer might demand special bodywork, such as the bullion vans of Thomas Tilling or the Royal Mail vans of McNamara, while another would ask that the vehicle be of a certain make, for work was done for that manufacturer.

In another instance the contractor's whole fleet was employed on work for one customer - ICI Ltd. This was Lawton's Transport Ltd of Farnworth, Lancs which became 60C Kearsley group under BRS from 1949.

One of the problems facing hauliers employed on contract hire, was that at the end of a contract the vehicle might well be of little use for other work, having been built specially for the contract. In some cases it might be possible to do a quick repaint and send it out on other work, but in some cases the specialist bodywork was not compatible with general haulage.

With so many haulage companies being involved in contract hire, BRS set up a number of locations dedicated to the particular service under the heading of Contract Hire, this continuing until 1954 when BRS (Contracts) Ltd was created.

The following selection of photographs show some of the vehicles operated on contract hire, and illustrates the individual styles and types of the period.

Below: As an aid to publicity, BRS followed up the practice of many hauliers in loaning vehicles for carnivals, parades and festivals, where it was felt that it was for the benefit of a charity or the local community. In this instance the unusual step has been taken in providing a contract hire vehicle for the event, but it might have been done at the instigation of the customer, who managed more publicity than did BRS with their tiny notices that the vehicle came from Tunnel Avenue depot, SE10.

Left lower: Although "You Saw Them Everywhere", few looked like this. An 0-type 5-tonner with Neville tilt cab pictured at work for brewers Ind, Coope & Allsopp Ltd. Supplied by Manchester contractors Foulkes & Bailey, the thinking behind this design was to provide a semi-forward layout whilst retaining engine accessibility. The engine compartment was shielded from the crew, but a sizeable gap remained where the new cab front panel met the original Bedford radiator grille.

Above: With a BRS take-over of a haulier, often the first signs of the event was a new depot sign, and the appearance of BRS lions and wheels on the cab doors, or perhaps a new headboard or two. The wholesale repainting of fleets sometimes took years to achieve, especially if certain vehicles were earmarked for disposal. Many appeared without any fleet numbers in the early days, which was very frustrating when trying to decide where it was based. Most contract vehicles did not display a fleet number, and often it was painted on the inside of the cab. This photograph disproves that fact, for the Austin on contract for Symington's Soups displays both BRS crest and a fleet number on the cab doors. It was originally operated by Grants Transport of Higham Ferrers.

Left: Most unusual among the contract hire customers within the Transport Services group, was the Brighton Co-operative Society, whose motor fleet was supplied by Southern Transport Ltd. This 1935 Bedford 3-tonner. enjoying typical south coast holiday sunshine in the summer of 1948, was one of the fleet.

Left: Just to show that not all vehicles in the Transport Services group were large, this Austin K8 25cwt in service with a builders' merchants was supplied on contract by Southern Transport Ltd. A high sided truck body has been built on the Austin chassis/cab, and a padded frame attached to the nearside for carrying large sheets of glass. Note the 1940s shopfronts, particularly Stanleys Hairdressing Saloon, which is complete with a fine display of dummy cigarette cartons - what a collector's delight!

Below: The Thomas Tilling name goes back as far as 1847, and is better known for its history in 'bus operation. However Thomas Tilling Ltd once operated a large fleet of road haulage vehicles which were mostly on contract hire, but with some on general haulage. This rather veteran looking 30cwt Dennis van was one of a number of vans supplied on contract to biscuit manufacturers Macfarlane, Lang & Co. Ltd, and is built in the old style with a roof rack for the storage of empty biscuit tins. The Tilling fleet was based at a very modern depot in Searles Road, SE1. which was allocated as 9A by BRS.

Right: This Leyland 'Hippo' has a rather weary look to it, for it started service in 1935, and for many years had been on the Mackintosh contract. Originally in service with J.B. Brown of Peckham, SE15 it passed to 9A Searles Road depot, from where it operated with several more modern vehicles. It is pictured unloading at the Mackintosh-Caley London warehouse in Pentonville road in May 1952, where the driver has managed to position it right up to the front door!

Below: Most of the GEC fleet was operated on contracts with different operators in various parts of the country. This example was supplied on contract by the Glasgow Hiring Co. Ltd and it is not surprising that the local Albion chassis formed the basis. No need for a lightweight speedy vehicle in this instance, the reliable quality of the Albion chassis together with a substantial boxvan body provides a workmanlike outfit turned out in classic style for an important customer.

Left: One of the large contracts serviced by Thomas Tilling Ltd, was that for George Vickers Ltd, a firm of wholesale newspaper and magazine distributors. The contract called for vans with a capacity of about a ton, with reasonable headroom and accessibility, plus a fair turn of speed. With its overhead valve 28hp petrol engine, the Bedford K-type was certainly no sluggard, and the London area witnessed prompt pre-dawn deliveries of its reading matter.

Left: The Bedford S-type was well represented in the BRS fleet, in both rigid and articulated forms, but box vans were not so common. This 7-tonner was based at 9A Searles Road depot for a local paper producer, the product demanding a heavier capacity than usual because of the compact weight of paper in sheets or in rolls.

Right: The cheery driver asked to be included in any photograph of his trusty 'Octopus' which is turned out in the maroon livery of John Mackintosh of Halifax. This 1947 machine was one of a number of Leyland operated on the Mackintosh contract by J.B. Brown of Peckham, being originally allocated to Camberwell Group 7A Bellenden Street depot but later allocated to 9A Contracts depot at Searles Road. Upon acquisition in 1949, old No.10 which became 9A2473, had an unladen weight of 8ton 8cwt which allowed a payload of some 13ton 12cwt within the 22tons gross weight for this type of vehicle

Above: Most of the furniture vans acquired by the BTC were allocated to Pickfords for their Household Removals service, but this ageing Bedford was put into 9A Contracts depot when acquired from R.H. Sims of Margate. The reason for this was that BRS acquired the haulage contractor who had supplied the van on contract to Batchelars of Croydon. Batchelars themselves were a firm of furnishers primarily, and so outside the scope of the 1947 Act.

Right: One example of the Transport Services group contract hire services, is provided by this Austin K8 model van supplied on a C-hiring licence to a firm of bakers and caterers. Clues to the vehicle's identity are by the seven-pointed star on the cab door, and the C-disc displayed in the windscreen. The contractor's name, Henry Bayes Ltd is just about visible at the bottom of the cab door. Although the chassis and cab are of the original Austin Three-Way model, in this instance a plain van body with just rear doors has been specified by the customer.

Right: The Horace Marshall contract was of considerable size and the business demanded a vehicle of nominal capacity but with a turn of speed. The Bedford K-type fitted the bill at the time, for the capacity was adequate and the 28hp ohv petrol engine gave the vans a lively performance when the situation demanded.

Left: Turned out in the colours of book publishers George Newnes Ltd., this 2ton Austin was one of the large contract fleet of N.M.U. Ltd otherwise known as Northern Motor Utilities, based in York. First registered in September 1919, the company acted as general carriers providing regular services to the main centres of population in England, as well as operating a transport clearing house for other carriers. The company later became a subsidiary of Rowntree & Co. the confectioners, who used the vehicles for retail deliveries as well as supplying vehicles on contract for other traders. As early as 1929 it claimed a fleet of 180 vehicles, with 2½ acres of covered depot area in York together with branches in London, Trafford Park and Birmingham. In the mid 1930s the fleet totalled 280, rising to 330 by 1939, by which time additional branches at Liverpool, Hull, Cambridge, Gateshead and Leeds had opened.

Left: It needed a keen eye to spot some of the contract vehicles, for this R.J. Weeks Bedford luton van in the colours of Jacoll Hats, carried a very small fleet number and owner's name on the cab door. One clue to ownership was the painting of the registration number, for in those days a proper reflective number plate was not obligatory, and careful study could detect the artistic craft of the signwriter. This 1947 O-type was supplied on an A-contract licence, and under BRS control the Waterden Road-based Weeks fleet became 63A Hackney Wick group.

Above: The R.J. Weeks Ltd business was mainly in contract hire and meat haulage, and at the time of acquisition by the BTC the company had a fleet in excess of 300 vehicles. The vehicles were mainly of Albion manufacture, with a few Leylands, just five Internationals but with a growing number of Bedfords purchased in the years following the war. This Albion CX1 model was one of several vehicles supplied on contract to Canning Town Glass Works Ltd, and is seen with its load of clear glass bottles being roped down. According to the BTC AQ3 form, the vehicle was first registered in March 1939, and the Weeks fleet was documented for nationalisation in April 1949, but the 1930s Dyson trailer was not listed at the take-over. The R.J. Weeks contract hire fleet went on to form part of 63A Hackney Marsh group.

Right: The Metropolitan Transport Supply Co. Ltd was first registered in October 1927, being set up to provide a transport service for provision merchants Kearley & Tonge Ltd, replacing another haulage company which had been supplying vehicles on contract. First details mention a fleet of 150, but by the time operator licensing was introduced in the mid 1930s, the fleet was said to be 500-strong operating under an A-licence. This style of operation was useful in that all manner of goods for associate companies might be carried, but with the threat of nationalisation looming, the company was decidedly nervous about the outcome and asked the BTC for a guarantee that their business and customers would not suffer. As well as a large fleet under the M.T.S. Co. name, a number of useful contracts were obtained, this 7V Ford in Castrol livery being one. Under BRS control the contract fleet went to 70A Victoria Park group.

Right: The east London brewers Taylor, Walker & Co. Ltd operated a mixed fleet, with some vehicles being actually owned by the company, while others were supplied on a contract hire basis by Chas. A. Wells Ltd, who were based in E2. This 1932 Leyland was one of the Chas. Wells vehicles which passed to BRS in 1949, the Unit being classified A9. Our photograph shows the vehicle making a delivery to the Duke of Cambridge in West Green Road, Tottenham in September 1951.

Left: A 1950s style Commer Superpoise operated unusually by 66A Stratford group, probably because of the location of the original contractor.

Below: One of the Charles Wells contract vehicles, which became part of 70A Victoria Park group fleet. A notable case of a very specialised vehicle designed for a specific task. Turned out in bright yellow, these vehicles were certainly eye-catching in their day, and BRS maintained the contract for some time. One example of the special bodywork which was not suitable for general haulage at the end of the contract period.

Left: After using some FG Foden and Leyland 'Octopus' types for the Whitbread contract, BRS chose to use some rather drab looking AECs as the business declined. This example was new to BRS, and was photographed near the depot in Power Road, Chiswick which was specially built for the contract in 1935.

Overleaf: A page from an early issue of the BRS Magazine, giving details of the contract fleet operated from 60C Kearsley group. The upper photograph shows the later vehicles taken into service by BRS, while in the lower workshop view it is possible to pick out some of the older DG Fodens which were part of the original fleet of Lawton's Transport Ltd, acquired in 1949.

C 60

Kearsley Group of Manchester District, North-Western Division, is a Contracts Group operating 112 vehicles engaged solely on haulage work for Messrs. Imperial Chemical Industries Ltd. The activity centres on the Dyestuffs Division, but C60 caters also for a considerable amount of traffic for the other Divisions of I.C.I.

The traffic hauled by Kearsley vehicles consists mainly of chemicals in various forms, from liquids in bulk to the finished product ready for delivery to the customer. It includes nylon polymer, nitric acid, caustic soda liquor, soda ash and paint.

Our fleet consist of six- and eight-wheeled machines, both tankers and platform-bodied, and many of them incorporate special features and modifications made or added in the workshops which are an integral part of the Group premises. All vehicles are painted in the customer's livery. Operations cover Scotland, south-eastern and south-western England, the north-eastern areas, Lancashire and Yorkshire. The operating schedules run often cover a full twenty-four-hours cycle (owing to the special nature of the commodities carried) and this raises particular problems of working schedules, change-over, etc. Not the last of these problems is that of preventive maintenance as the customer, most understandably, insists on a high standard of appearance for these vehicles which are themselves a "running advertisement."

The premises were acquired in 1949, with 67 vehicles, from Lawton's Transport Ltd., and are among the most up-to-date establishments in North-Western Division. The Group is completely self-contained, in that it undertakes major engineering tasks, body building, painting and lettering.

Our photographs give some small indication of the type of fleet operated, and of the facilities available at C60

APPENDICES

F. Allen Ltd.
Banning Street, Greenwich SE10.

B & G Transport
Wood Street, Peterborough.

David Barrie Ltd.
East Dock Street, Dundee.

A.C. Bell & Sons Ltd.
Seamer, Scarborough.

Burrough & Sons Ltd.
London Road, Stanford-Le-Hope.

C. & L. Transport Ltd.
Ettingsall Road, Wolverhampton.

F. Carr & Son Ltd.
Dean Street, Bedford.

Charlish & Price Ltd.
Pultney Mews, Bath.

Thos. S. Charnell Ltd.
Wolverhampton Road, Bentley, Walsall.

C.A. & F. Cook Ltd.
Bromley Street, Hull.

Fred Darby & Sons Ltd.
Sutton Ely

H. & R. Duncan Ltd.
Lower Gilmore Place, Edinburgh.

A & J. Dunn Ltd.
West Borland, Denny.

Elliott's Transport Ltd.
Alexander Road, Newport.

J.T. Elwell Ltd.
Wolverhampton Road, Bentley, Walsall.

Gordon & Sons Ltd.
Stakeford, Choppington.

Greenwoods Transport Ltd.
Ramsey, Huntingdon.

Guest, Wood & Ling Ltd.
Locksbrook Road, Bath.

A.J. Gupwell Transport Ltd.
Well Lane, Birmingham.

R. Harrison Ltd.
London.

Hepplewhite & Shaw Ltd.
Low Row, Sunderland.

Hinchcliffe Ltd.
Pitt Street, Sheffield.

Hughes & Beattie Ltd.
Carleton, Carlisle.

Imperia Transport Ltd.
York Street, Manchester.

S. J. Jeffrey Ltd.
Swansea.

Jennens Brothers Transport Ltd.
Jockey Road, Sutton Coldfield.

Joint Transport Ltd.
Seamer, Scarborough.

H.W. Jones Ltd.
Cromwell Road, Wisbech.

John Lampard Ltd.
West Harnham, Salisbury.

Lansdowne Motors (Cardiff) Ltd.
Canton, Cardiff.

S. Latham & Sons Ltd.
Groby, Leicester.

Longbridge Transport Ltd.
Lodge Road, Redditch.

Marshall Brothers Ltd.
Knowsley Road, St. Helens.

F. Marshall & Son Ltd.
Granite Wharf, Banning St, Greenwich

Mason & Son Ltd.
Wood Street, Peterborough.

Medway Transport Ltd.
Pump Lane, Rainham.

Miller & Co. Ltd.
Water Street, Liverpool.

John Morton & Son Ltd.
Hertford Street, Coventry.

John & R.C. Nixon Ltd.
Station Road, Tunstall, Stoke-on Trent.

North Staffs Haulage Co. Ltd.
Hamill Road, Stoke-on-Trent.

O.K. Carrier Co. Ltd.
Weaver Street, Leeds.

W.T. Parrott & Co. Ltd.
Dunstable Road, Luton.

Fred. Robinson Ltd.
Church Road, Stockton-on-Tees.

Charles Scott's Road Service Ltd.
Turl Street, Oxford.

Springfield Carriers Ltd.
York Street, Manchester.

Swindon Transport Ltd.
Drove Road, Swindon.

Talbot Transport Ltd.
Stone, Kidderminster.

Road Haulage Ltd.
Lovaine Place, Wallsend.

Warrington's Transport Ltd.
Eyre Road, Sheffield 1.

R.T. Watson & Son Ltd.
Locksbrook Road, Bath.

William Wiseley & Sons Ltd.
Virginia Street, Aberdeen.

George Wood Transport Ltd.
Barn Street, Birmingham.

The Structure of BRS

GENERAL HAULAGE

The BRS general haulage operations were based on a Division, District, Group system. There were eight Divisions, each having a Divisional colour code.

Division	Colour Code	Group (Max)
A. South East	Royal Blue	44 Groups
B. Scottish	Traffic Blue	27 Groups
C. North Western	Sea Green	31 Groups
D. North Eastern	Road Haulage Red	36 Groups
E. Midland	Nut Brown	36 Groups
F. South Western	Road Haulage Green	19 Groups
G. Western	Lead Grey	14 Groups
H. Eastern	Torquoise Blue	24 Groups

The Divisions were divided into Districts, and the Districts in turn divided into Groups. The exception to this structure being the South East Division which was divided into Services rather then Groups.

The Districts had no identification system allocated to identify them within a Division but the Groups were identified within their Division; the Group number preceding the divisional identifying letter, e.g. '3B' was the identification sequence of the Peterhead/Fraserburgh Group (3), within the Scottish Division (B).

Vehicles carried a sequence number which incorporated both the Division/Group reference and its own individual fleet number within the Group, e.g. the AEC 'Mammoth Major' illustrated on page four carries the identification sequence '3B10'. This indicates that the vehicle is no.10 within the Peterhead/Fraserburgh Group.

At first, the 'Lead Companies' - sizeable limited companies usually voluntarily acquired, being generally former RHO units and which formed the nucleus of BRS* - mostly operated under their former titles, with addition of (BTC) before the Ltd at the end of the name.

*See page seven for further information. The Lead Companies' are also identified by bold lettering in the list of BRS undertakings commencing on page 151.

From 1st April 1953, all vehicles carried only the name of the Group, although the word 'Group' was now being omitted. The vehicle fleet number was also repeated with black letters on the white background on the rear of the vehicle.

Reorganisations, at the completion of the major part of the compulsory acquisition programme and as a consequence of the impending denationalisation programme, led to a number of changes in the structure, not least the abolition of the District tier. The effect of these changes is shown in the list of BRS undertakings in italics.

At its peak, General Haulage comprised 231 Groups. Each operating up to 200 vehicles from several depots.

Unless otherwise detailed in the listing of undertakings, all the traffic was described as General Traffic - either Local or Trunk Services; generally night trunk to depots, with day drivers/shunters for the local work.

Note: In the list of BRS Undertakings where an undertaking had a depot in another division, the divisional code of the undertaking's main operating centre is shown before its company name.

CONTRACT HIRE

The Contract Hire undertakings acquired continued to be operated as separate depots by BRS, and in 1954 BRS Contracts was created. This allowed it to compete with private enterprise operators. This it did with success.

In the South East 'A' Division, where the bulk of the contracts were, the Contract Services depots continued to be based on the former acquired undertakings;

CONTRACTS at 1951

SOUTH EAST 'A' DIVISION

9A Newington Butts, Searle Road SE1.	Thomas Tilling.
42A Shoreditch, Curtain Road EC2. **sub-depots**; Bermondsey, SE16, Great Ormond Street, WC1	
49A Finsbury EC1. **sub-depots**; Epworth Street EC2. Westminster Bridge SE1.	MacNamara.
51A Chiswick W4.	C.D. & T. Contracts.
52A Perivale **sub-depot**; Tulse Hill SW2.	N.M.U.
63A Hackney Wick. Waterden Road E15	Weeks.
70A Victoria Park E2. **sub-depots**: Cambridge Heath E15. Tredegar Square E2.	Chas. A. Wells.

SCOTTISH DIVISION

Glasgow 6B	Taylors

Contract Hire continued

NORTH EASTERN DIVISION
62C Manchester Contracts.   ex Foulkes & Bailey;
Trafford Park,   N.M.U.

WESTERN DIVISION
2G Cardiff Contracts   ex Foulkes & Bailey
Ely Depot.

MIDLAND DIVISION
5E Aston Cross Group   ex Pickfords
Dartmouth Street.

PARCELS & SMALLS

Those undertakings whose principal traffic was Parcels and Smalls were placed in a separate Parcels section, with its own Deputy Chief Officer. The largest acquired parcels undertakings were to remain as virtually autonomous units until after 1953.

SPECIAL TRAFFICS. ST(P).

This was the ninth Division. It absorbed any special traffics previously operated as a part of an acquired undertaking operating nationally. The Division was based on the former Hays Wharf, Pickfords Companies and became:

PICKFORDS REMOVALS & STORAGE
London Area : Home Counties Branch

Finsbury Park. N4.   London 20 Branches;
    H. Counties, 53 Branches

South Western Area

Cotham Hill, Bristol.   42 Branches
    (at 1953, 48 Branches)

Midland Area

Castle Boulevard, Nottingham.   36 Branches

Northern Area

Marsh Street, Bradford.   51 Branches
    (at 1953, 59 Branches)

Scottish Area

Bishop Street, Glasgow.   13 Branches

HEAVY HAULAGE
London, 4 Depots:

Park Royal, NW10.   Enfield.

Stratford, E15.   Tower Bridge Road, SE1.

Provincial Depots:

Barrow-in-Furness.   Birmingham.

Birtley,   Bristol.

Cardiff.   Co. Durham.

Exeter.   Glasgow.

Heavy Haulage, provincial towns continued

Hull.   Ispwich

Kings Lynn   Leicester
(closed by 1953).
Lincoln.   Liverpool.

Manchester   Derby

Peterborough   Sheffield.

Stafford.   Walsall
(At 1953 depots also existed at Doncaster, Edinburgh, Preston, Rugby, Stockton-on-Tees).

PICKFORDS TANK HAULAGE

London.   Bromborough,
    (Cheshire).
Hull.   Liverpool.

Manchester.

MEAT CARTAGE
London:
Poplar.   Smithfield.
    (By 1953, 7 Branches)
Provincial Depots:
Bath.   Bournemouth.

Birmingham*.   Bootle*.

Bristol.   Glasgow*.

Liverpool*.   Leeds*.

Manchester*.   Newcastle-on-Tyne*.

Portsmouth.   Southampton*.

Southend-on-Sea.
(By 1953 Liverpool depot was closed for Meat, and depots opened at Avonmouth and Doncaster)*.
    *Indicates that these were also heavy haulage depots.

CONTRACTS & MULTIPLE SHOP DELIVERIES
Multiple Shops Deliveries was established in 1932 to service the shops of the Home & Colonial Group which included Maypole Dairies, Liptons, Pearks and Meadow Dairies. Household names also featured in the contracts fleet with vehicles in the colours of Dunlop, Marks & Spencer & ICI. This specialised element of Pickfords' pre-nationalisation operations was to remain within the control of the ninth division during the early years of BRS covered by this book.

Multiple Shop Depots:
London, Long Lane.   Bootle.

This listing of groups and depots/units shows the earlier, major acquisitions existing at 1949/1950. When an address is shown without a name of an acquired undertaking, this is because no positive record is known. The 'Lead Companies' (see page seven) are in bold.

The listing was compiled from BRS directories and lists, from records in the trade periodicals of that period, and from the observations of enthusiasts. Because of the rapid expansion - followed by changes due to political decisions - the details of the Groups at 1953 are included, except for Division A. South East.

Some early closures of depots occurred when purpose built or refurbished depots were opened, e.g. Bristol, Wordsley, and Hull.

A. SOUTH EASTERN DIVISION

Boundaries: London; Middlesex; Kent; Sussex; Essex; Hertford (south of a line approximately Markyate, through Ware and Ongar to Malden (excl. Ingatesone); Surrey; Bucks (south of and including Aylesbury); Berks, east of a line from Twyford to approximately Blackwater.

SOUTH EASTERN DIVISION - PARCELS

A3. Waterden Road, E15	Bouts-Tillotson.
A16. Seward Street	Holdsworth & Hanson.
A19. Whitecross Street.	Sutton
A34. Goswell Road	Carter Paterson.

GENERAL HAULAGE GROUPS - four Districts at 1950.

The reorganisation following the completion of the major part of the acquisition programme and then the impending denationalisation led to changes.

SOUTH EASTERN DISTRICT 1A-9A.

1A EAST KENT GROUP.
To be transferred becoming 60F EAST KENT (CANTERBURY).

Depots: 1 Wincheap, Canterbury:	C.& G. Yeoman.
Deal:	Blunt.
1/3 Park Road, Cheriton:	South East Roadways; Edwards & Son (Transport) Ltd.
Minster:	White, Sims

2A MID KENT GROUP.
To be transferred becoming 61F MID-KENT (MAIDSTONE).

Depots: Bearsted:	Tolhurst.
Larkfield:	**Thomas Tilling.**
Sutton Road, Maidstone:	**Kent Carriers**; Phillips Motors; L.E. Wright
Marden:	Tippen.
Branbridges, Paddock Wood:	Arnold
Tonbridge:	Ashline; Harpers.
The Square, Yalding:	Monkton Transport.

3A NORTH WEST KENT GROUP.
Traffic: General, Timber.

Depots: Bexley Heath:	Clarkes Transport; Essex; L. & E. Transport.
Charlton:	H.O.K.Transport; Hewstone
Dartford:	Frost.
Eynesford:	Brown.
Swanley:	Harber; Smith.
14/17 Woolwich High Street SE18:	**Tuff & Hoar.**

4A MEDWAY GROUP.
To be transferred becoming 62F MEDWAY (STROOD).

Depots: Holborn Wharf, Medway St. Chatham:	**Gammon & Dicker.**
Doddington:	Brenchley; Elvey'sTransport.
Key Street, Sittingbourne:	Barrett; Brenchley; Elvey; Farm Factors; Ferrell.
Rainham, Pump Lane:	Gammon & Dicker; Medway Transport.
Bill Street, Frindsbury, Rochester:	Atkins; Nicholls.
Sheerness:	Clay; Welby's Transport.
Sittingbourne:	Standen.
Strood, Priory Road:	Gammon & Dicker: Arthrell.

5A BLACKWELL TUNNEL GROUP.
Traffic: Local, Cables.
Trunks; Leicester, Nottingham

Depots: Creekside SE10, (Granite Wharf, Banning Street):	**Marshall**; Allen; Colley's Transport; J.Guemans.
Greenwich SE10, (Christchurch Way):	Carters Transport; King & Sparrow
New Cross SE14, (Kerry Road, Lewisham):	Hodge; May; E. Paul
Tunnel Avenue SE10, (Blackwall Lane):	Broad & Montague.
Deptford:	(E)Annable; (E)CastleTransport; (E)Latham; (E)Fred Edlin; (E)Groombridge; (E)Kinders Transport; (E)Painter; (E)Robin Hood; (E)Wortley & Clifford.

6A BERMONDSEY GROUP.
Traffic: General: Directional;
Trunk Liverpool, B and D Divisions.

Depots: Dockhead, Druid Street SE1; London Bridge	Cook. (C)Guest; (C)Heaton; (C)E.Hucks; (C)Motor Carriers; (C)Rose; (C)Taylor & Otter.
Rotherhithe:	(G)All British Carriers; (F)Ashley Down; (E)Crooke; Jolins; (F)Knee Bros; (F)Newlands; (G)O'Sullivan.
Neckinger:	(D)Acme Transport; (D)Cook; Gammon & Dicker. (D)OnwardTransport; (B)London Scottish (D)Robinson; (D)Smith.
Surrey Docks, Silwood Street;	(B)Barrie; (B)Cowan; Gammon & Dicker (B)London Scottish; (C) Miller; (B)Smith.

6A BERMONDSEY GROUP (continued)

Tower Bridge (Tooley Street):	(E)Everett Transport;
	(E)Gupwell;
	(E) Jennens Transport.
East Road;	L.W. Ward

7A CAMBERWELL GROUP.

Depots: Peckham (Benhill Road SE5):	Blows; Botton & Goodrham;
	Hutchinson;
	Pierson, Middleton;
	Richardson; Wallaker.
Denmark Hill:	Dales.
Kennington Park SE5,	
(184 Camberwell New Road):	Bowler & Mack.
Old Kent Road:	Barnards; Clarkes; Pooley.
Walworth:	Richardson.
Sub-depots: Kennington Park:	P.D.Q. Tpt.
Old Kent Road:	(C)Cadman;(C)Foley; (E)Green;
	(C)Longton; (C)Morris;
	(C)North Staffs Haulage.
Peckham:	(D)Wheelhouse; Brown

8A ROTHER VALLEY GROUP.

To be transferred becoming
63F ROTHER VALLEY (TENTERDEN).

Depots: Ashford, Woodford Road,	
Kingsnorth:	Ashford Transport;
	Sutton; Hoasewood
Battle:	L. O. Blain Beney.
	General and Local
Hailsham:	Langford.
Headcorn:	Blackman; Charlton;
	Fermor; Smith.
Rye:	Jempson; Joy.
Tenterden:	Judge.

9A NEWINGTON BUTTS.

Traffic: General, Directional; E Division.

Depots: Victory Place,	
(Balfour Street SE1):	**S.J. Mengenis.**
Searle Road SE1:	**Thomas Tilling.**

SOUTH WESTERN DISTRICT.
20A, 23A, 25A-27A, 29A

20A BRIGHTON GROUP.

To be transferred becoming 64F BRIGHTON
Traffic: General, Contracts.

Depots: 17/56 Warwick Street,	
Brighton:	**Southern Transport**;
	Grover; Hardy.
Kemp Town, Brighton:	Pownall.
Haywards Heath:	Cook.
Kemp Town:	Colgate & Gray; Pownall
Free Wharf, Brighton Road, Shoreham:	Coast Transport; Redman;
	Smarts.
Wivelsfield Green:	Dinnage.

23A CROYDON GROUP.

Depots: Lansdowne Road:	Gilchrist.
Stafford Road:	Purley Way Motors;
	Triggs & Chapman.
Kingston:	A. Ewart Bristow.
Barnham, Station Hotel Yard,	
Bognor Regis:	Barnham Transport Co. Ltd.

23A CROYDON GROUP (continued)

Aldingbourne, Nyton Road:	Dutton; Russell.
Kingston-on-Thames,	
205/207 Kingston Road:	Dallas & Co.(Transport) Ltd;
	A.C. Hemus.
Morden & Cheam:	Excevis & Tooting; Jeffery;
	Lewis; Savory Bros.
New Malden:	Adams.
Walton-on-Thames:	A.H. Price.

25A BATTERSEA GROUP.

Traffic: General; Trunk; Oxford.

Depots: Battersea,	
32 Battersea Bridge Road:	Munday; Witheys.
Brixton, Mandrell Road SW2:	Dutfield.
Southwark, 26 Southwark Bridge Road:	
	Ashcroft;
	Southwark Garage; Taylor;
	Witheys.
Sub-depot:	(E)Craddock;
	(C)Dallas, Leyland;
	(C)John Meeks; Spiller.

26A GUILDFORD GROUP.

Traffic: General, Contracts.

Depots: Guildford: 4 Mangles Road:	
	H. Rackliffe; Ward.
SR Goods Station,	Chaplin.
Traffic: Railway Cartage.	
Chertsey:	Minns.
Dorking:	Apps; Peacock.
Pirbright, The Green:	Henden.
Shere:	Smith.

27A LAMBETH GROUP

Depots: 27 Great Guildford Street:	Ashcroft.
Centaur Street SE1.	H. & G. Dutfield.

29A BOROUGH

Traffic General,
Trunk F Division; London.

	Routh and Stevens.
	Dawson

NORTH WESTERN DISTRICT. 40A-53A.

40A St. ALBANS GROUP.

Depots: St. Albans; Hatfield Road:	Currell & Rand; N.H. Dunn,
	(merged with (C)N. Dunn);
	(C)Gregson; Kia-ora.
Victoria Street:	Rand.
Park Garge, Rickmansworth:	Wrights Transport
	(Herts) Ltd.
Kings Langley; 1 Alexandra Road:	(E)Appleford; Sammons;
	Sunderland
London Colney:	(C)GerrardsTransport;
	Currell & Rand
Watford:	Sammons.
Welwyn Garden City:	Barnes.

41A HIGH WYCOMBE GROUP.

Traffic: General, New Furniture,
Timber.

Depots: High Wycombe;	
Copy Ground Lane:	Dean.
Frogmore:	T. & B. Road Services.

41A HIGH WYCOMBE GROUP (continued)

Marsh:	Baker.
Richardson Street:	Mealing.
Aylesbury: Aston Clifton Road:	Willis Carriers

Traffic: Dairy, Produce, Grain, General

Chesham:	Griffett & Collis.
Princes Risborough:	Hickman.
Amersham:	Gordon Lee

42A SHOREDITCH GROUP.

Traffic: New Furniture; Contract; Foodstuffs; Fruit.
Depots: Shoreditch EC2:

87/89 Curtain Road:	**Henry Bayes**.
181 Drummond Road:	
Rivington Street:	J. Eva
Fore Street:	Enfield Haulage.

43A ISLINGTON GROUP.

Traffic; General; Directional; Brick & Tiles; New Furniture; Timber.
Depots: Camden Town,

6 Castle Road:	Thos. Smith.
Kentish Town:	**General Roadways**.
Kingsland Road:	(C)A.H. Barlow; (C)Lloyd; (D)Mason; (C)North Western Transport Services; (C)Radcliffe & Sackville.
Cornelia Street, Arundel Garage N7:	Steve Eastmead.
Enfield:	(C)T.A. Barlow; (C)Lawrence; (C)Moffat Roadways; Lea Valley Transport.

Sub-depot: Shaftesbury Street N1;

New North Road:	F.C. Baker.

44A TOTTENHAM GROUP.

Traffic: General; New Furniture.
Depots: Tottenham N1;

Balls Pond Road:	Glibbery; Greenbow; Osborn; Osborn; Bert Whiting.
Tottenham N1, High Cross:	Goddard
Hawley Road NW1:	Lea.
Holloway:	Chapple.
Sherborough Road N15:	Wade.

45A BRENTFORD GROUP.

Depots: London Road, Brentford:

	(C)Ballards; Cliffords Ltd; (F)Hutton; Ideal; Potter & Potter; Universal.
Park Royal:	Cliffords; Greenwood.
Silvertown	Macks.

46A SLOUGH GROUP.

Traffic: General; Timber.
Depots: Alpha Street, Slough;

	Janes and C. & B. Transport; Johns.
Bracknell:	J. Slade.
Marlow:	Tillion.

47A CITY GROUP.

Depots:

	(C)Cartage; Joseph Eva.

48A HAYES GROUP.

Traffic: General; Machinery; Long Loads.
Depots: Cubitt Town;

	Burgoines (part).

48A HAYES GROUP (continued)

Springfield Road:	Adamson; Burgoines (part);
Etherington;	(G)Hereford Haulage; Parrish.

49A FINSBURY.

Depot: Epworth Street EC1:

	McNamara; A.H. Barker; (C)Buckley; Franks of Old Street; (C)Knowles; (C)Melias; (C) Ward; (C)Warpool; (E)Weatherhogg.
Brixton;	

50A MUSWELL HILL.

By 1951 Parcels Division
Depot: Coppetts Road:

	Fisher Renwick; Bellingham; C.A.R.T; (D)Chesterfield Transport; (E)Kelling; Lawrence; Majestic Roadways; Millard; (C)Rawson; (D)Turnbull.
Paddington, The Wharf, Amberley Road W9:	

51A CHISWICK.

Depot: Power Road W4:

	C. D. & T Contracts.

52A PERIVALE GROUP.

Depots: Walmgate Road:

	(D)Northern Motor Utilities.
Edgware:	Taylor.
Church Lane, Kingsbury NW9:	C. Lacey.
6/12 Tulse Hill SW2.	
Wealdstone:	Harrow & Wealdstone Transport.

53A WEST LONDON.

Traffic: General; Theatre Scenery; Refrigerators.
Depots: Acton:

Acton:	Smith & Ward.
Dock Road E16	T. Mileham
Fulham, Carnforth Road SW6:	Stirling Haulage, Young's Garages.
Hammersmith: Great Church Lane W6:	
Harlesden:	Austin; Crownhill.
Shepherds Bush, Goldhawk Road;	(F)G. Baker & Sons; Coales; Cooper; Collins & Stevenson; P.L.P. Motors; Southern Roadways; A.H. Wood.

NORTH EASTERN DISTRICT.
60A-66A, 70A, 71A-74A.

60A BOW GROUP.

Depots: 59 Central Street, EC1:

	Davis Haulage Ltd; Hacker; Igerton; Lovell; Prince; Risdon Semper; Ardley; Egerton; Goddard

Note: transferred from 44A Poplar and named Bow Group. The fleet was then dispersed to other Groups.

127/131 Bow Road E3:	G.W. Transport.

60A BOW GROUP (continued)

Clare Street:

Bradbrook;
(H)East Anglia Transport.

Holley Wharf:
Hopson.

7 Moreton Road E3:
Dowling.

Caspian Wharf, Violet Road E3:

61A THURROCK GROUP.

Depots: London Road,
Stanford-le-Hope: Burrough Ltd.
Brentwood, High Street: Bragg.
London Road: Bloomfields.
Grays, London Road: Harris.
Traffic: Tipping
Rayleigh: Grimwades; Patten.
West Street, Romford: Collis.
Romford: Holmes.
Upminster Road, Upminster: Gidden.

62A BISHOPGATE.

Depots: Hadleigh Street: Kahan.
Leith Road, Bow E3:   Cox.
Salmon Lane E14:   Claridge Holt; Hilliard; Paul;
     Roberts.
Wheler Street: **Kneller & Chandler**;
     Watson.
Sub-depot: St. Pauls Way E3:   Rushbrook Transport;
     Transcarrier.
Stanstead Abbots: Hawkins.

63A HACKNEY MARSH GROUP.

Depot: Waterden Road E15:   Weeks.

64A MONUMENT GROUP.

Traffic: Fruit and Produce. Local,
Docks, to and from Markets.
Depots: Bethnal Green,
Paradise Row E2:   Reece; Terminal Transport;
     (H)Toby Transport.
Spitalfields: Jacobs; Read.

65A MILLWALL GROUP.

Depots: Canning Town: Simpson.
Emmett Street E14:   Blomfield; Watson.
Havanah Street E14:   Huish.
Sub-depot:
Klondyke Garage,
West Ferry Road E14:   Ardley;
     (E)C. & L. Transport;
     Eslick.
     (E)John Morton & Son Ltd;
     (E)Partridge;
     (E)Toft Bros & Tomlinson.

66A STRATFORD.

Traffic: General. Trunk: Bristol.
Depots: Chobham Road: Warne.
Dock Road E16:   Mileham.
Lett Road E16:   Woodcock.
Martin Street: Rockman Brothers.
West Ham Lane: Mayes.

70A VICTORIA PARK GROUP.

Traffic: General, Building Materials.
Depots: 260 Cambridge Heath Road E2:
     Chas A. Wells.
Orchard Place: Baker.

71A EAST HAM GROUP.

Depots: Barking: Bank; South Dock Haulage.
Watson Ave E6:   East Ham Haulage; Miller;
     Pattenden.
Woodford: Wright.
Sub-depot: Wellington Road E6:   Holls; Moore; Whitehiose.

72A STEPNEY GROUP.

Traffic: General Haulage;
Cold Store Movements
Depots: Christian Street;   Fairclough.
Violet Road;   G.W. Transport
Jamaica Street;   Watson.
Cubitt Town;   Burgoyne.

74A EDMONTON GROUP.

Depots: Capworth Street,
Lea Bridge Road E10:   Bristow (part).
Carlton Road South: Sage Transport.
Clapton Common: Defries.
Dalston Lane: Bristow (part).
Eleys Estate: J.T. Contracts.
Felixstowe Road N17:   D. S. Roadways; Taylor.
Lamb Lane: Donnelly.
Medway Road, Bow: Winner Motor Transport.
Odessa Road: Bishop; Hammerton;
     Red Transport.
Waverley Road N17:   Crawley.
Sub-branch: Ferry Lane N17:   (B)Duncan;
     (B)Regal Transport.

B. SCOTTISH DIVISION

ABERDEEN DISTRICT 1B-5B

1B ABERDEEN GENERAL GROUP.

Traffic: Local and Docks,
General B Division
Depots: 28 and also 56 Virginia Square:
     G. Abel;
Chas. Alexander;   J.G. Barrack Ltd;
     Brechin Road Transport;
     John Davie;
     Elliot & Hutcheon;
     Munro's Motor
        Transport Ltd;
     Mutter Howey & Co. Ltd;
     W. Philip Transport Ltd;
     Universal Transport Co;
     Wm.Wisely; Wordie & Co.
Sub-depots: Roger's Walk Garage.
Holland Street: Mutter Howey & Co.
Also at 1953: Inverurie; Station Road, Laurencekirk,
Traffic: General, B; Local, Aberdeen City; Stonehaven.

2B OLD FORD ROAD (ABERDEEN) GROUP.

Traffic: Fish, also General;
England and Scotland.
Depots: Old Ford Road &
Summerfield Terrace: Chas. Alexander;
     Munro's Motors.
Sub-Depots: James Street.
Traffic: Aberdeen: Local and O.B. parcels.
     Wm. Wisely.

2B OLD FORD ROAD (ABERDEEN) GROUP (continued)

Aberdeen, King Street:
Traffic: General: Aberdeen; Forres; Inverness; Nairn.
Mountholy:
Traffic: General: Aberdeen; Dundee;
Fifeldy; Kinross; Perth; Stirling; Speyside.
Summerfield Terrace.
Traffic: General and Smalls.
Willowdale Place: W. & R. Murray; Transport Ltd.
Auchenblae; Woodside.
Traffic: General.
Ballater; Rosslyn Cottage.
Traffic: General.
Banchory; Raemoir Cottage.
Traffic: General.
Buckie; Garden Lane.
Traffic: Fish, Aberdeen; General,
Livestock. All Divns.
Dufftown: York Street:
Traffic: General.
Elgin; Panspot Street.
Traffic: General.
Forres; Tullend Lane.
Traffic: General.

3B PETERHEAD/FRASERBURGH GROUP.

Depots: Fraserburgh; Albert Street.
Traffic: General, Fish, Livestock, Machinery; All Divns.
Peterhead;
Traffic: Fish; Trunk; North West Ports to Aberdeen.
                                    Peter Sutherland.
Ellon; Station Road.   Eddie; French & Gibb.
Also at 1953: now NORTH EAST SCOTLAND GROUP:
Buckie; Fraserborough; Huntley; Macduff;
Portsoy; Newdeer; Turriff.

4B BUCKIE GROUP.

Not listed 1953.
Depots: 2 Fish Market, Buckie: P. Sutherland;
                                    W. Taylor.
Blackfriars Road, Elgin: Chas. Alexander;
                                    MacKechnie & Buchan;
                                    J. Morrison.
Huntley: A. Gray;
                                    Munro's Motor Transport.
Macduff: Chas. Alexander.
Portsoy: Cruikshank Bros.
Turriff: Munro's Motor Transport.

5B INVERNESS GROUP.

Depots: 1 Eastgate, Inverness: Wordie & Co.
also at Forres, Thurso & Wick.
Dingwall; Conon Bridge: **D.McLennan & Co.**;
                                    Smith Bros (Inverness).
Craigellachie: Speyside Transport.
Fraser Ross;
Brook Rockfield Mill, Fearn: Wordie & Co.
Sub-depot: Alness; Averon Garage.
Traffic: General.
Also at 1953: Elgin; The Pier, Gairloch (Agent); Inverurie;
Nairn; Newtonmore; Portmahomack; Ullapool; Wick.

6B ABERDEEN PARCELS.

DUNDEE DISTRICT 20B-25B

20B DUNDEE GROUP.

Also at 1953.

20B DUNDEE GROUP (continued)

Traffic: General; Trunk; Manchester,
Preston, London. Tipping; Local
Depot: 54 East Dock Street, Dundee: D. Barrie Ltd; Carrie & Sons;
                                    Davidson Transport Ltd;
                                    Fisher Renwick;
                                    (C)J. & E. Transport Ltd;
                                    J. Moffat; Tay Motor Lorry Co.

Sub-depot: 10 Mile Street.
22 Rosebank Street: Duguid Mills.

21B ANGUS GROUP.

Traffic: General; B.
Depots: Arbroath; Ladyloan:
Traffic: General.
Aylth; New Road: D. L. Mitchell (Meigle) Ltd;
                                    M.L. Thomas.
Brechin; Commerce Street: J. C. & W. Christie;
                                    C. Hanton.
Forfar; Robert Street:
Traffic: General, Agricultural
and Tipping. All Divns.
                                    D. Callender; A. Melville;
                                    Ritchie Brothers; Wordie & Co.
also Montrose.
Also at 1953: ANGUS (FORFAR): Miegle; Montrose.

22B PERTH GROUP.

Also at 1953.
Depots: 10 Mill Street, Perth: Wordie & Co.
St. Catherines Road, Perth: J.D. Burns; R. Nichol & Co:
                                    Wilks Bros.
Mill Street, Aberfeldy: Youngs Express Deliveries.
Sub-depot: Aberfeldy; Central Garage: Guy Bros.
Depot: Blairgowrie; Haugh Road:
Traffic: General
                                    J. Dehelm. Prain Bros;
                                    Wordie & Co.
Sub-depots: Crieff; 7 Gavelmore Street:
Traffic: General and Livestock.
                                    P. Halley.
3-5 Fues, Auchterarder: J. Bayne.
Coupar Angus; Queen Street: Wordie & Co. Ltd.
Sub-depot: Union Street.

23B NORTH FIFE (LEVEN) GROUP.

Depots: Cupar; Provost Wynd:
Traffic: General and Livestock.
                                    F.J.Bowerbank; A. Muir;
                                    W. Oliphant.
Glebefield Works, Leven: C. Adamson; J. Birrell & Son;
                                    J.R. Carmichael Ltd.
                                    A.N. Leggate; J. Williamson.
Wellesley Road, Methil:
Traffic: General B only.
                                    W. Murdock Ltd.
Mansdale, Strathkinness: Chas. Alexander; M.B. Danskin;
                                    C. Wilson (Pittenwen) Ltd

24B SOUTH FIFE (DUNFERMLINE) GROUP.

Also at 1953.
Traffic: General.
Depots: Kelliebank, Alloa: Cowan & Co; J.J. Gordon;
                                    Keddie Transport.
Alva; Brookfield Garage:
Ramblingwell, Dunfermline:
Traffic: General all Divns;
Manchester Trunk.
                                    Aitkin (Lassodie); Cowan & Co.
                                    Mutter Howey & Co. Ltd;

24B SOUTH FIFE (DUNFERMLINE) GROUP (continued)

Ramblingwell, Dunfermline (cont): D. West & Son.
Kirkaldy; Victoria Road: Youngs Express Deliveries;
Mutter Howey & Co. Ltd.

Sub-depots:
Alloa; Grange Road.
Dunfermline; Bruce Street:
Oakfield Garage, Kinross: W. Nelson.
Oakfield Garage, Kelty:
Traffic: General and Livestock.

A. & A. Young.

25B TAY GROUP.
Not listed 1953.
Traffic: General B only.
Depots: 98 Albert Street, Dundee: Dickson's Tayport Ltd;
D. Horsborough;
E. Robertson & Co. Ltd;
Whtye Bros.
South Union Street, Dundee: Mutter Howey & Co Ltd;
Wordie & Co.

At 1953: 25B DUNDEE PARCELS.

EDINBURGH DISTRICT 40B-45B

40B EDINBURGH GROUP.
Traffic: General; Household Removals,
all Divns; Trunk, London, Vans only.
Depot: Lower Gilmore Street 3: **H. & R. Duncan**;
Halley Deliveries.
Sub-depot: 15/23 Ratcliff Terrace 9: Paterson Bros. (C.M.H) Ltd., &
Paterson Bros. (R. & S.)Ltd.

At 1953: EDINBURGH (GENERAL): Edinburgh 6;
Leith; Newhaven. Household Removals to Pickfords.

41B LEITH GROUP.
Not Listed 1953.
Depots: 8/10 Bernard Street, Edinburgh:
Traffic: General C, D, F, G Divns;
and West Midlands;
Trunks to Birmingham, Leeds,
Liverpool; Manchester, Newcastle.

Cowan & Co.

248 Eastern Road, Edinburgh:
Traffic: General and Smalls, B only.

Mutter Howey & Co. Ltd.
52 Lorne Street, Leith: Scottish Parcels.
Marine Gardens, Portobello: J.D.Banks & Co;
J.R. Carmichael Ltd;
C.G. Macintosh.

Fishmarket Buildings, Newhaven:
Traffic: Fish only.

R. Brand & Son;
J. Carnie & Sons;
D.Dryborough;
T. Smith Jnr;
J.F. Young.

At 1953; 41B EDINBURGH PARCELS.

42B WAVERLEY GROUP.
Depots: 63/65 Polton Street,
Bonnyrigg: W. Hunter;
J. Renwick & Son.
Sub-depot: Pennycuick 4: J. Watson.
Gylemuir Road, Costerphine, Edinburgh:
Traffic: B; Part-loads, Directional;
Tipping, Local.

H. Davidson:
W.G.D. Pollock;
R. Sharp & Sons.

42B WAVERLEY GROUP (continued)

93 Albert Street, Leith 6: Cowan & Co. Ltd;
Mutter Howey & Co Ltd;
Wordie & Co.
20 Baltic Street, Leith:
Traffic: General B; Trunks; Aberdeen,
Dundee, Glasgow.

Alex. Smart;
T. W. Davidson Jnr.
Sub-depot: 117 Pitt Street, Leith 6:
Traffic: General, B only

A.C.S. Motors.
15 Tower Street, Leith 6: G.R. Robb (Transport);
J. Robertson;
F. Saddler & Co. Ltd.
Warehousing Department: 36 Constitution Street, Leith.
At 1953: EDINBURGH (WAVERLEY):
63/65 Polton Street, Bonnyrigg; Berwick Street,
also Tower Street, Leith, Musselburgh.

43B WEST LOTHIAN GROUP.
Traffic: General B only; Directional,
Full loads All Divns; Part Loads, England only.
Depots: Guildiehaugh, Bathgate:
Traffic: General B only,
Milk and Livestock.

A.C. Carroll (Bathgate);
Mutter Howey & Co. Ltd;
J.W. Petrie; J.& J. Philip;
W. Russell.
Sub-depots: Main Street,
Braehead, Lanark: W.G.D.Pollock (Carnwith);
Hartwood Road,West Calder: J. Russell & Sons Ltd.
46/48 Register Street, Bo'ness:
Traffic: General B; Full Loads all Divns;
Part Loads, appropriate groups.

W.H. Boyd;
Cochrane's (Bo'ness) Ltd;
J. McAvoy.
Stockbridge, Linlithgow: **W. Aitken & Co**.
Mutter Howey & Co. Ltd.

At 1953: WEST LOTHIAN (LINLITHGLOW):
Bellabeg; Bo'ness; and Linlithglow.

44B EAST LOTHIAN GROUP.
Depot: 14 Cort Street, Haddington: Guy Bros;
G. Paterson & Sons Ltd. (part).
Sub-depots: Dunbar; Central Garage.
Traffic: B, Parcels and Smalls,
Full loads Direct;
Part loads, appropriate Group;

Starks Motor Carrier Service.
Greenlaw: W. Middlemiss & Sons.
181 North Street, Haddington:
J. Arnott (Musselburgh);
A. Nicol & Co. Ltd;
G. Paterson & Sons Ltd (part).
At 1953: EAST LOTHIAN & BORDERS (HADDINGTON):
Haddington: Dunbar, Galshiels; Hawick; Kelso; Peebles.

45B BORDERS GROUP.
Not Listed 1953.
Depots: Galashiels; Ludhope Vale:
Traffic: General and Livestock, all Divns.
2 Sime Place: J. Arnott;
Mutter Howey & Co. Ltd.
Sub-depots: Earlston, Westfield Road:
Traffic: General and Smalls,
Daily; All Divns;
Trunks, Edinburgh, London, Manchester.

W. Rodger & Sons.

45B BORDERS GROUP (continued)

Greenlaw; Marchmont Road:
Traffic: General and Smalls, all Divns.
Hawick; Main Street:

T. Cairns;
Mutter Howey & Co. Ltd.

Lauder; 15 West High Street:
Traffic: General and Livestock, all Divns;
regular to Leith, Leeds, Leicester.

G. Paterson & Sons Ltd. (part).
Selkirk; Ladybank Garage:
Mutter Howey & Co. Ltd.
Northgate Garage, Peebles:
A. & W. R. Little;
Penderleith & Stevenson;
Youngs Express Deliveries.

Depot: Sheddon Park Road, Kelso:
Mutter Howey & Co. Ltd;
J. Turnbull (Kelso) Ltd;
Turner Bros; Weatherson.

GLASGOW DISTRICT. 60B, 62B-69B.

60B GLASGOW GROUP.

At 1951 GLASGOW (DOUGLAS) GROUP.
Depots: 367 Alexandra Parade E1:
Traffic: General, Dundee and Aberdeen.

Universal Transport.

Midland Street C1:
Traffic: General and Heavy Haulage.

I. Barrie.

46 West George Street C2;
Traffic: General B, not Argyllshire;

P. Saddler & Co. Ltd;
Wordie & Co. Ltd.

65/73 South Harbour Street, Ayr:

E. Ferguson Ltd.

Sub-depots: Ayr; Agricultural Hall,
Dam Park:
McGawn.
Ayr; 10 Alloway Street:
E. Ferguson Ltd;
Moores Motors.
Girvan; Royal Hotel Garage:
McKechnie's Motors.
Maybole; Ailsa Garage, Seaton Road:
Dunabie.
Depot: 54 Irvine Road, Kilmarnock:
D. Mckinnon.
Sub-depots: Camerons Buildings,
Crosshouse:
J. Clews.
34 Boyd Street, Kilmarnock:
John McColl.
Maybank Garage, Kilmarnock:
J.H. Livingstone;
1/3 Thistle Street, Stirling:
A.C. Carroll; Wordie & Co. Ltd.
At 1953: DOUGLAS (GLASGOW); Greendyke Street, Glasgow C5;
Kessock Street C4; North Wallace street C4; West Street C5;
At 1953 see also 69B AYRSHIRE (KILMARNOCK)

61B SCOTTISH PARCELS.

62B CLYDE GROUP.

Depots: 96 Admiral Street, Glasgow: G.C. McIndoe Ltd.
40 Carmichael Street SW1:
Traffic: Local, Docks, Tipping; General;
Greenock and Edinburgh.

F. Smillie & Son.

113/117 Elliot Street C3:
Traffic: Local, Docks;
Greenock and Edinburgh.

A.C.S. Motors.

25 Weir Street C5:
Traffic: Local, Docks. General;
Greenock and Edinburgh.
Greenock; 52 Regent Street.
Traffic: Local, Docks. General Edinburgh.
46 Wellington Street: Church (Transport) Ltd.
4/6 Orchard Street, Paisley: A. Duncan.
At 1953: Carmichael Street SW1; Elliot Street C3;
Weir Street C5; Greenock; Paisley.

63B LONDON SCOTTISH GROUP.

Traffic: General; A; B, C, D
not Newcastle; E, H. Rippenden.
Depots: Riverside, Alloa;
Carfin Road, Holytown; London Scottish Transport.
2/12 Albert Street, Motherwell.
Sub-depots: 12A Stein Square,
Bannockburn: London Scottish; J.D. Ward.
70 Main Street, Doune: J. Bremer; London Scottish.
Canderside Garage, Larkhall: D.M. Smith.
Depot: London Road Garage,
Mount Vernon: J. Hadfield, J. & E. Transport.
Sub-depot: 180/186 Stewartson Street,
Wishaw: J. Skene.
Depot: 1 Robertson Street, Glasgow: Regal Transport Co.Ltd;
Southern Transport
Sub-depot: Busby, Clarkston: Jenkins Express.
At 1953: LONDON SCOTTISH (C2): Ligler Street Glasgow C4;
Mount Vernon C2; Station Road, Law; Waverley Street,
Coatbridge; Motherwell: Wishaw.

64B WALLACE GROUP.

Traffic: To connecting Cowan's depots;
Trunks to London, and F; G only
Depots: 80 North Wallace Street C4: **Cowan & Co**.
26 Clyde Street: **London Scottish**.
At 1953: WALLACE (C2): North Wallace Street.

65B TAYLOR'S GROUP.

Traffic: Contracts; Local.
Depots: 2/4 Portree Street, A.Taylor & Sons.
Sub-depot: 21 Carmichael Street W1.
Roman Bridge, Dunochar, Clydebank:

G. Davies & Son Ltd.
Also at 1953: TAYLOR (C2): Ardrie Street C4.

66B ARGYLL GROUP.

Depots: 17 Tylefield Street, Glasgow SE:
Traffic: General; outwards to Argyllshire.

Argyll Transport Ltd.

Sub-depot: Bellfield Street E1;
Traffic incoming from Argyllshire.

Clyde & Campbeltown
Shipping Co. Ltd;
Gareloch Transport.
Wellclose, Campbeltown: J. Hule & Co;
Kintyre Road Services.
Strone; Tyneshadon: Wm. Mitchell (Strone) Ltd.
Sub-depot: The Garage, Lochgilphead:
Bellfield Street, Glasgow: Wm. Mitchell (Strone) Ltd.
At 1953: ARGYLL (C2): Warroch Street, Glasgow C3;
Campbeltown; Inverary; Lochgilphead; Oban; Strone; Tarbert.

67B CENTRAL SCOTLAND GROUP.

Traffic: General A, E, and H Divns; T
runk to Luton.
Depots: Viewfield, Cumbernauld: **A.C. Carroll**;
White Line Tranport.

Sub-depot: Falkirk Road, Larbert:
Traffic: General A, E, and H Divns;
Trunk to Luton.

London Scottish Transport Ltd.
Also at 1953: CENTRAL SCOTLAND (DENNY):
Depots: Barn Garage, Bainsford;
West Borland, Denny: A. & J. Dunn Ltd.
Falkirk; Garage, Grangemouth Road,
Dock Lye Sheds, Junction Dock,
Grangemouth; Stirling.
Sub-depots: 29 Quackerfield, Bannockburn:
20 Main Street, Doune.

68B CALEDONIAN GROUP.
Depots; Abington; Exhibition Garage:
Traffic; General, mainly Livestock.

Youngs Express Deliveries.

Castle Douglas; Creetown;
B.R. Goods Yard, Dumfries:
Whitesands:
Dickson;
Dumfries & Galloway
   Transport;
Hunter.

Sub-depot: Eastfield Road:
(C) Caledonian.
Traffic; General; Daily Glasgow;
Strone; Wigtown.
Claythorne Street, Glasgow C5.

(C) Caledonian.

Traffic: Smalls; Glasgow, Dumfries,
Strone, Wigtown.
Gretna; Victory Avenue.
Traffic: General.
Kirkcudbright; Dee Walk.
Traffic: General.
Lockerbie; Townhead Street:
South Western.
Traffic: General, Mainly Milk.
Polnackie; Seafield Garage.
G. Halliday.
Stranraer; Lewis Street.

69B AYRSHIRE GROUP.
At 1953, formerly part of GLASGOW (DOUGLAS) GROUP.
Depot: Ayr:
MacGawn;
E Ferguson;
Moores Motors.
Darvel; Central Garage:
Andrew Smith.
Girvan; Royal Hotel Garage:
McKechnie's Motors.
Kilmarnock; 34 Boyd Street:
D. McKinnon;
John McColl.
Maybank Garage:

J.H. Livingstone
Maybole; Seaton Road:
Dunable.

C. NORTH WESTERN DIVISION
BOUNDARIES at 1949: Lancashire; Cumbria; Westmorland;
Flintshire; Anglesey; most of Denbigh and North Caernarvon;
Merioneth; and parts of West Yorkshire; West Derbyshire.

LIVERPOOL DISTRICT. 1C-8C, 11C-12C.

1C NORTH LIVERPOOL GROUP.
Traffic: General; Trunks to D,E,F,G.
Depot: Crosshall Street 1:
Harding Bros Transport Ltd;
E. Shoesmith;
G.W. Wood.

At 1953: Pierhead and Vulcan Street.

2C CENTRAL LIVERPOOL GROUP.
Traffic: General; Trunk London.
Depots: Old Hall Street 3:
Bennetts Haulage,
Warehousing &
   Wharfage Co;
General Roadways;
Lewis; Union.
Crosby Road South 21:
Trunk: General; Glasgow and B.

(B)J.R. Carmichael & Co.
76 Sefton Road, Litherland 21.

Stevenson Transport.
Also at 1953: Chapel Street 20; Victoria Street 2.

3C SOUTH LIVERPOOL GROUP.
Trunk A and F Divns.
Depot: Water Street:
Miller & Co;
Liverpool Cartage Co. Ltd;
Handscombe;
Sir Thomas Street:
Feather & Kent.
Ellesmere Port, 56/58 Dock Street:
O.B. Transport.
At 1953: South Castle Street 1: Warrington.

4C EAST LIVERPOOL GROUP.
Depot: 31 Little Wooton Street 7:
Forkings; Riverside Motors;
Taylor; C.S. Walker.
Tithebarn Street:
Motor Carriers.
At 1953: Little Wooton Street 7; Studholm Street 20.

5C WARRINGTON GROUP.
Traffic: General; Trunks, London,
Birmingham, Bristol, Coventry,
Liverpool, Norwich.
Depots: Runcorn, Station Road:
Woods Motors.
34 Stanley Street:
Jackson & Ellis.
Warrington, 28 Forshaw Street:

Bailey.
57-59 Knutsford Road:
De Burgh Transports; Lewis
Mersey Motor Engineers.
Sutton Street:
Whitehall.
Vernon Street:
(A)Ardleys; (A)Hacker;
(A)Lovell;
(A)Risdon Semper.
Linkside:
(A)Gaults; (A)Jardine: (A)Prince.
at 1953: Ellesmere Port; Stockton Heath.

6C St. HELENS & WIDNES (St. HELENS) GROUP.
Traffic: General;
Trunks to Birmingham, Evesham,
Manchester, Potteries.
Depots: St.Helens, Albion Road:
Davies & Brownlow.
Ellan Head Road, Sutton Heath:
A.B. Sutton & Sons.
7 Lea Green Road:
McKinnell.
Knowsley Road:
Marshall.
Sherdley Road:
Robert Heaton & Sons.
Widnes, Irland Street:
At 1953: Also Widnes, Birchfield Road: B. & B. Haulage Co.

7C WIGAN GROUP.
Traffic: General.
Trunk to London, Liverpool,
Manchester, Newcastle-on-Tyne.
Depot: Wigan, Hindley,
Wigan Road:
Millgate:
J. Farr & Co.
Skelmersdale; 17 Sandy Lane:
Gregson.
Also at 1953: Atherton; Blackrod, Bolton.

8C NORTH WALES GROUP.
Depot: Abergale, Trem Y Tur Garage:
Chester, Bretton, Premier Garage:

Arthur Hughes;
Shepherd & Hughes.
Also at 1953: Bellsale; Bodelwyddan

9C LIVERPOOL PARCELS.

11C MID CHESHIRE GROUP.
Traffic: General. Trunks; London,
Liverpool, Manchester.

11C MID CHESHIRE GROUP (continued)
Depots: Northwich, Lostock Gralam: P.L. & S.G. Harris;
A. Leicester.
Sandbach, East Elworth Garage: Lovell,
Jones,
Whittaker.

Fourways Garage, Arclid:
Traffic; General; Livestock and Meat.
Trunks to London, Glasgow,
Liverpool, Norwich.
Tarporley, Tilstone Garage:
Traffic; General;
Trunks to Liverpool, Cheshire,
Shropshire, Potteries, North Wales. Esply.
A.E. Handcombe & Co. Ltd.

Also at 1953: Northwich

12C LIVERPOOL PORT. Central Organisation
Depots: Birkenhead, Kings Dock, Liverpool;
North John Street 2: Seacombe.

LANCASTER DISTRICT. 21C-26C

20C LANCASTER PARCELS (BURNLEY).

21C BURNLEY GROUP.
Depots: Burnley, Canning Street: Burnley Reliance Transport.
62 Standish Street: Wesley Clegg.
Gannow Top, Burnley Road:
Traffic; General; Trunks; Glasgow,
Carlisle, London, Preston, 'D'. Colne,
Hyde Park Garage, North Valley Road:
Traffic; General; Trunks to Liverpool, **F. Allum**;
East Lancs, Newcastle. Wm. Feather & Sons.
Daniel Platt: Riding.
Longridge, Farnells Transport;
Nelson, Carr Road: H. Pilkington.
8 Higson Road: Wesley Clegg.
Padiham, Burnley Road:
J.H. Dickenson;
Feather & Ombler;
G.F. Foster;
E. Marsden;
Pollard Bros;
Richardson Transport.

At 1953: Clitheroe; Cornholme, Todmorden.

22C PRESTON GROUP.
Traffic: General.
Depots: Leyland, Earnshaw Bridge: Dallas Services Ltd
Preston, Water Lane: **Viney & Co. Ltd**;
John Walker.

*Also at 1953: Blackpool; Carlisle; Albert Edward Dock
and Walton-le-Dale, Preston.*

23C CARLISLE GROUP.
Traffic: General and Livestock.
Depots: Gilerux; Johnston Bros.
Carlisle, Durran Hill Road: Robson.
Carleton:
Traffic: General and Livestock.

Cockermouth. **Hughes & Beattie**.
 Traffic; Tipping. Nicholson.
Harraby: Thistle Transport Co.
Also at 1953: Howgate; Penrith.

24C WEST BLACKBURN GROUP.
Depots: Bennington Street: Hardmen & Gillibrand.
Stansfield Street:
Traffic: General
also Perishables; London.
W.H. Bowker.
Adlington, Babylon Lane:
Springfield:
Also at 1953: Darwen, Oswaldtwistle.

25C MORECOMBE BAY (LANCASTER) GROUP.
Traffic; General; Trunks, East Lancs;
Yorks, West Riding; London.
Depots: Barrow-in-Furness,
Hindpool Road:
Lancaster, Brewery Lane Garage; Fred Milner.
Ulverston, Priory Road; Athersmith Bros.
Workington, Winscales: Cumberland Roadways.
*Also at 1953: Barrow-in-Furness;
Kendal: Lancaster; Staniforth.*

26C ROSSENDALE (ACCRINGTON) GROUP.
Also at 1953.
Depot: Accrington, Burnley Road; **Ashworth Heys**.
Ramsbottom, Whalley Road: Stringfellow.
Rossendale, Rawtenstall,
Bacup Road Garage:
Traffic: General,Cloth,Storage. A,B,C,D
(W. Riding & S. Yorks only).
J. & E. Transport.

MANCHESTER DISTRICT
60C-62C, 64C-70C, 73C-74C.

60C KEARSLEY GROUP.
Depot: Farnworth. Hipwood & Grundy.
Depot: Farnworth Lawton
Traffic: Imperial Chemical Industries only
At 1953: KEARSLEY (FARNWORTH)

61C NORTH MANCHESTER GROUP.
Depot: Cecil Street, Greenheys M15:
Trunks; London.
A.H. Barlow (Transport) Ltd.
Cheadle, Brook Road: Booth.
Cheetham, Thomas Street: Holden.
*At 1953: Alderley Edge; Glossop; Macclesfield;
No8. Dock, Salford; Stockport.*

62C MANCHESTER CONTRACTS GROUP.
Depot: Trafford Park: **Foulkes & Bailey**;
Northern Motor Utilities.
Also at Temperence Street M12.

63C MANCHESTER PARCELS.
White City: **Fisher Renwick.**

64C GREENHEYS (MANCHESTER) GROUP.
Depots: Swinton Hall Road, Swinton: Gerrards Transport.
Wentworth, Wentworth Street M12.
Stockport, Wellington Road South

65C SALFORD GROUP.
Not listed 1953.

65C SALFORD GROUP (continued)

Depots: 2 Cross Lane 5:   Allen; Autocarriers.
12, East Ordsall Road 3:   North Western
             Transport Services.
Cheetham, 102 North Street: A.E.G. Transport.

66C CENTRAL MANCHESTER GROUP.

Not listed 1953.
Depot: York Street: A.E.G. Transport; Lake;
Springfield Street;   H. Swain & Co.

67C TRAFFORD PARK GROUP.

Depot: Ashburton Road: Williams; Smith.
Also at 1953: Bolton; Richmond Street Manchester M17;
Third Ave M17; Rochdale.

68C MANCHESTER LOCAL GROUP.

Not listed 1953.
All J. Nall.
Traffic: Railway and General Cartage.
Depots: Corporation Street M6.
Bolton, Manchester Road Goods Yard.
Bury, Knowsley Street Goods Yard.
Chorley, Salisbury Street Goods Yard.
Darwen, Lodge Bank Goods Yard.
Hindley and Wigan Goods Yard.
Hollinwood, Spencer Street Goods Yard.

69C BOLTON & BURY GROUP.

Depot: Bolton, Four Lane Ends;   A.H. Barlow.
Kay Street: Melias; H.F.W. Transport.
Bury, Back Parsons Lane: Etheridge.
Brierley Street: (A)Allied Freight Services.
Fox Street: Direct Haulage; Eastham.
Chorley, Whittle Springs: Lowe & Coxehead.
Also at 1953: BOLTON & BURY (BOLTON);
Darwen; Blackstock Street, Liverpool;
Oldham; Radcliffe; Salford.

70C OLDHAM GROUP.

Not listed 1953.
Depot; Hamilton Road: Barnes.
Spencer Street;   Cusick, Gladwick.

73C SOUTH MANCHESTER GROUP.

Not listed 1953.
Depot: Trafford Park M17.

74C CORNBROOK GROUP.

Depot: Chester Road:
Traffic to Cowan's connecting depots.
     (B)Cowan.
Also at 1953: CORNBROOK (MANCHESTER);
Ratcliffe; Salford.

D. NORTH EASTERN DIVISION

Boundaries at 1949: Northumberland; Co. Durham; Derbyshire
(portion south of Sheffield, including Chesterfield).

TYNE/TEES DISTRICT. 1D - 9D.

1D CENTRAL NEWCASTLE GROUP.

Trunk to A and F Divns. Machinery,

1D CENTRAL NEWCASTLE GROUP (continued)

Traffic (cont): Meat, Contracts.
Depot: Morton Street: McPhee; Green; Oliver;
     F. Willinson;
     J. Younger.
28/30 Moseley Street: **Tyne Ferries.** (C)Feather.
The Side: Jameson Garage:
Traffic: General and Meat.
Trunk, Hull.
Stepney Road: Dickinson Transporters.
North Shields: Burgess.
Also at 1953: The Close, Newcastle.

2D HAYMARKET NEWCASTLE GROUP.

Depot: Newcastle, Bethel Avenue 2:   North British Roadways.
Lovaine Place: **Wallsend Haulage**.
Blaydon-on-Tyne, Garden Street: P. & R. Transport;
     Wyatt Transport.
Also at 1953: HAYMARKET (NEWCASTLE);
Haltwhistle; Hexham; Quayside, Newcastle.

3D GATESHEAD GROUP.

Not listed at 1953.
Traffic: General.
Depots: Abbot Street:
Trunks: Birmingham.
     Waltons.
Team Valley T. Est, Second Avenue:
Trunks; Edinburgh, Glasgow,
Hull, Manchester.
     Northumbrian Transport.
Town Street: **Robson**; Robinson.
Birtley.
Traffic: General, Regular Trunk, B (Lowlands only),
C (excludes Liverpool).
     Atkinson.
Felling-on-Tyne, Imperial Garage:
Trunks: Liverpool, Manchester, Glasgow.
     Blaney.

4D STOCKTON GROUP.

Depots: Middlesborough, Clarendon Road:
32 Cleveland Street: Harrison's.
Trunks, Hull, Bradford, Leeds,
Tyneside. Queens Square.
Trunks; London,Teeside,
Tyneside. Stockton, Bridge Road: **Waltons.**
Church Road, Central Garage: **Fred Robinson**;
     Lamb; Walters;
Station Garage:
Trunk, Birmingham.   Williamson.
     (C)Feather & Kent.
Thornby, Stockton Road: Bee-Line Roadways
At 1953: TEESIDE (STOCKTON); Barnard Castle;
Bishop Auckland; Darlington; Middlesborough;
Chapel Street, also Wilson Street, Thornby-on-Tees;
West Hartlepool; Yarm-on-Tees.

5D MIDDLESBOROUGH GROUP.

Not listed 1953.
Traffic: General.
Depots: Dinsdale,
Fighting Cocks Garage: Lamb.
Langley Moor, High Street Garage:
Trunk, London.
     R. Gardner, Milner,
     Oliver & Sinclair.
North Ormsby, Cleveland Garage:
Trunks, Liverpool, Manchester.
     Teeside Motor Transport.

6D SUNDERLAND GROUP

Depot: Holmside: Peter Wilkinson.
Low Row:
Trunks, Grimsby, Hull.

                                Brown & Harrison;
                                Hepplewhite & Shaw.
East Stanley, 47 East Street: Seymour Bros.
Monkwearmouth,
Strand Street Garage: Thompson.
Also at 1953: South Shields;
also Silksworth Row, Sunderland.

7D QUAYSIDE NEWCASTLE GROUP.
Not Listed 1953.
Depot: Quayside: J. Baxter. G. Gowland:
                                Joseph M. Prior;
                                Jos. Reah.

8D SANDYFORD NEWCASTLE GROUP.
Depot: Berwick-on-Tweed, College Place:
Traffic: General & Agricultural Materials,
B. and D Divisions.

                                J. Whillis & Son;
                                D. & B. Davis.
Choppington, Stakeford:
Traffic: General C. General and Electric Cable
B and D Divisions.
                                Gordon.
Also at 1953: SANDYFORD (NEWCASTLE);
Fella; Durnsddle Street, Seahouses, Wooler.

9D EXCHANGE NEWCASTLE GROUP.
Not Listed 1953. Transferred to 8D SANDYFORD (NEWCASTLE).
Depots: 15 Queen Street 1:   **F. Short & Sons**.
Bedlington,
Half Moon Garage;

10D TYNE/TEES PARCELS.

LEEDS, YORK & EAST RIDING DISTRICT.
20D, 22D-29D.

20D YORK GROUP.
Depots: Bridlington: Old Town:
                                Bell;
                                Joint Transport.
Normanton, Gilcar Street: J.R. Holme & Co;
                                Toft Bros. & Tomlinson.
Ripon, 25 Market Place: Rumfitt's.
Seamer (Scarborough),
Stocks Hill Garage:
York, Fetter Lane: Bell; Joint Transport,
Walmgate Bar: Northern Motor Utilities.
Also at 1953: Harrogate.

22D NORTH LEEDS GROUP.
Depot: Kirkstall Road 4:
Trunks; London, Birmingham, Coventry,
Wolverhampton.
                                O.K. Carrier Co.
Sayner Road, Hunslet;   R. Barr (Leeds) Ltd;
                                W.H. Fish & Sons Ltd;
                                Harrison.
Pudsey, Grove Garage, Cemetery Road: **Hudson**, Kaye.
Also at 1953: Kirkstall Road, also Neville Street,
Leeds; Meanwood Street, Pudsey.

23D SOUTH LEEDS GROUP.
Depots: Water Lane, Leeds 11:
Rothwell, Wakefield Road:
Regent Garage:
Bell Hill, Wood Lane: Bramley;
                                  Grimshaw;
                                  Parker.
Also at 1953: Corner Park Road, also Marshall Street, Leeds; Wakefield.

24D CENTRAL LEEDS GROUP.
Not Listed 1953.
Depots: 31 Grase Street: Harries.
Whitehall Road 12.

25D CENTRAL HULL GROUP.
Not Listed 1953. Absorbed into 28D.
Traffic: General; Local; Horse(drawn) Transport; Timber.
Depots: Blanket Row: Ramsey;
                                Richardson Carriers;
                                Wells.
27/31 Bright Street: Bays Horse Transport.
Clough Road: Bays Motor Transport;
                                Hewitt Transport.
Hyperion Street:
Trunks, Birmingham, Liverpool.
                                A. Norman Annison;
                                Barrick & Fenton;
                                Marshall's Motors.
Leeds Road: Rushworth Swain.
Walton Street: North Western
                                  Transport Services.
Wellington Street:
Traffic: General. Trunks: E. Yorks; C and D Divns.
                                (C)Harding.

26D SELBY GROUP.
Traffic: General
Depot: Aberford, Main Street Garage: Aberford Transprt.
Ackworth, 92 Wakefield Road:
Traffic: General, Agricultural Products
as required.   **Ackworth Transport**;
                                Clewly.
Castleford, Malt Kiln Lane: **Castleford**
                                Transport Co. Ltd.
Selby, Holme Lane: **Onward Transport**.
Also at 1953: Goole; Knottingley.

27D NORTH HULL GROUP.
Traffic: Trunks:
Newcastle; A. D. E and H Divns:
Depot: Bromley Street: **C.A. & F. Cook**.
Leeds Road: Acey.
Myton Street:
Pickering Road: **Fred Cook (Transport) Ltd**.
Market Weighton, Holme Road:
Traffic; Also Sugar Beet.
At 1953: also Southcote Lane, and Walton Street Hull.

28D EAST HULL GROUP
Depots: Clarence Street:
Scott Street: Hodgson.
South Street:
Hedon: Brooksbank.
At 1953: Clayton Road, also Edwards Place,
Hyperion Street, Oxford Street; Wellington Street
and Wincomlee, Hull.

29D LEEDS, YORK & EAST RIDING PARCELS (YORK).

WEST RIDING DISTRICT. 40D-47D

40D HALIFAX GROUP.
Depots: Brighouse, Atlas Mill Road: **Butterwick & Walker.**
Mytholmroyd, Stocks Garage: Moss.
Also at 1953: Elland; Horton Street,
also Union Street South, Hailfax.

41D RIPPONDEN GROUP.
Depot: Hebden Bridge: Hebden Haulage Co.
Ripponden Garage: **Beaumont Bros.**
The Triangle: Hutchinson.
Also at 1953: Ovenden.

42D HUDDERSFIELD GROUP.
Depot: Holmfirth: Parkhead Garage.
New Mill, The Garage: Booth.
Nile Street:
Traffic: General and Smalls.

       Queen Carriage;
       Kirkby.
Outlane, The Garage: Gee.
Paddock, 9 Branch Street: Ellis.
Slaithwaite:
Trunks to Edinburgh, Glasgow, Hull,
Ipswich, Newcastle, and 'H' Divn.

       Francis & Brook.
At 1953 also Milnsbridge.

43D SOUTH BRADFORD GROUP.
Depot: Leagrave Road, Bradford.
177 Thornton Road: Bell; Crow;
       Tranship.
At 1953: Northbrook Street and Ventnor Street, Bradford.

44D CENTRAL BRADFORD GROUP.
Not Listed 1953.
Depot; 16 Leeds Road: **Blythe & Berwick**; Long.

45D AIREDALE GROUP.
Depot: Bingley, Alice Road: Butterfield.
Main Street:
Trunks; Hull, Liverpool, London.

       Forder.
Keighley, Dalton Lane: Conyers.
Greenwood Street: Fowlds, Langton.
West Lane:
Trunks; London, B,C,and E Divns.

       Bonnett;
       Keighley Transport.
Also at 1953: AIREDALE (BINGLEY): Goods Station,
also Albion Garage, Keighley Road, Keighley.

46D DEWSBURY/BATLEY GROUP.
Traffic: General B. E Divns. Trunks to Hull, Liverpool; London,
Southampton; Yarn, Textiles, Machinery, Wire.
Depot: Batley, Bulrush Garage,
Bradford Road West: Bailey Bros.
Crown Garage, Bradford Road: Liversedge, Oldroyd,
       Tranship.
Dewsbury, Savile Town: **Bowyer & Jackson.**
Also at 1953: DEWSBURY/BATLEY (BATLEY): Batley;
Cleckheaton; Mill Street East, also Scout Hill, Batley.

47D WEST BRADFORD GROUP.
Also at 1953.
Depot: Wakefield Road, Bradford.

SOUTH YORKSHIRE DISTRICT. 60D-68D.

60D CENTRAL SHEFFIELD GROUP.
Depots: 20/42 Albert Road: Finnegan,Wheeler,
       Woodseats.
104 Bradfield Road: Arthur Hinchcliffe.
103 Doctor Lane: T. Smith.
80/88 Eyre Lane:
Trunks; London, Birmingham.

       Warrington Transport.
428 London Road: G.F. Phillips.
108 Mansfield Road 2:   **Sedgwick.**
Pitt Street, Portland Lane: **Hinchcliffe.**
Rutland Road 3:   **Trowbridge.**
Also at 1953: also Star Garage, Penistone Road:
Glossops Transport.

61D CHESTERFIELD GROUP.
Transferred from 65E DUKERIES GROUP 1951.
Traffic: Metal Box, Yarn from Bolton.
Depots: Whittington, Station Road:
Pass. Walton Road: **Chesterfield Transport.**

62D ATTERCLIFFE GROUP.
Depots: Anson Street: D162.
62D Attercliffe Group continued:
Rotherham, Sheffield Road.
87/97 Wilton Gardens: Yates.
Tinsley, Shepcote Lane: Geo. Picken; S. Harrison.
Also at 1953: ATTERCLIFFE (SHEFFIELD):
Fitzwilliam Street, Sheffield.

63D PARK GROUP.
Depots: Sheffield, Athol Road 8:
Trunks: London, Birmingham, Glasgow,
Leeds, Liverpool, Manchester.

       Gregory's Transport.
Worthing Road: John Grocock Ltd.
Also at 1953: PARK (SHEFFIELD):
Woodburn Road.

64D DONCASTER GROUP.
Depots: 58/60 Cemetery Street: Jackson.
Cooke Street: Earnshaw Richards.
10 North Bridge Road: Currie & Co.
Whitaker Street: Stamford.
Conisborough, Sheffield Road:
Also at 1953: Arnthorpe; Barnby Dam;
Spotborough Road, Doncaster.

65D BARNSLEY GROUP.
Traffic: General and Meat.
Trunks B Divn; Birmingham, Bristol,
London, Luton, South Wales.
Depots: Meadow Street: **Fisher.**
174 Pontefract Road, Curdworth: Mason.
Deane Garage, Hoyle Mill: Thompson Transport.
Curdworth, 174 Pontefract Road: **D. Mason.**
Wombwell, Woodside Garage: T. Rodwell & Son Ltd.
Also at 1953: Penistone.

66D HALLAM GROUP.
Not listed 1953.
Depots: Malin Bridge: Bramhall;
       Brind;
       Griffiths;
       Parker.
Penistone Road, Star Garage: **Glossops Transport.**

67D SOUTH YORKSHIRE PARCELS.

68D SHERWOOD GROUP.
Depots: Newark, Fardon, Fosse Road: Baldock Transport.
Worksop, 'The Roadways' Dock Road: Sergeants Transport.
Also at 1953: SHERWOOD (WORKSOP):
Dunham-on-Trent; Oldcotes; New Ollerton; Retford.

E. MIDLAND DIVISION
BOUNDARIES at 1949: Covers most of Derbyshire, Leicestershire, Northamptonshire, Staffordshire excluding the Potteries), South Nottinghamshire, Oxfordshire, West Berkshire, North Buckinghamshire, North Worcestershire, Shropshire. Modified 1951 to line from, but excluding Dore, Chester(excl), Chesterfield (excl), Nottingham, Rushden, Bedford, Luton, Aylesbury (excl), Kidderminster, Wolverhampton, Shrewsbury (excl), Whitchurch, Crewe.

BIRMINGHAM & COVENTRY DISTRICT
1E-6E, 8E-11E.

1E BULL RING GROUP.
Not listed 1953.
Depots: Allison Street: Geo. Wood.
Digbeth: Bellamy & Co;
(A)Broad & Montague;
(C)Greenwood Bros;
(C)Marshall Bros;
(A)Allen Simpson.
Well Lane: A.J. Gupwell.

2E COVENTRY GROUP.
Traffic: General. Trunks to London, Birmingham, Bristol, Liverpool, Manchester.
Depots: Harper Road: Economic Transport
& Trading Co. Ltd.
Quinton Road: **John Morton & Son**;
H. & H. Motorways.
J. H. C. Transport; Thos. Wise.
West Orchard: T. Mason; Partridge;
Clem. Varney; E.H. Brown.
Warwick Street, Earlsdon: A. W. Eagles.
Whitefriars Street: Langley & Wotton.
Leamington Spa, Russell Street: Leamington Spa Motor
Haulage Service Ltd.

At 1953 also London Road.

3E WITTON GROUP.
Not listed 1953.
Depots: Perry Barr, Davey Road 6:   L.J. Bassett;
Broadway Transport;
(B)Cowan & Co.
Jennens Brothes Ltd (part);
Stockland Garage;
(B)White Line Transport Ltd.
Butlin Street, Nechells 7;   S. Harris;
Jennens Brothers Ltd (part);
(A)Kneller & Chandler;
A.C.Leake;
A.Mason; (C)Motor Carriers;
(C)North Western
Transport Services;
(C)George Smith;
(D)J.W. Turnbull;
(D)H.L. Walker.
Lancaster Street 4:   H. Herringshaw;
(H)M. P. Transport;
Mansfield & Dawson.

4E CHEAPSIDE GROUP.
Traffic: London, Luton, BSA Tubes.
Depots: Cheapside: (A)Davies;
H.J.W. Portlock;
(A)Thomas Tilling;
T. Watson.
Watery Lane: (F)Downer & Co. Ltd;
(F)Southern Roadways.
Freeth Street, Ladywood: G. Bramfield.
White City, Aston Hall Road.   McNamara
At 1953 CHEAPSIDE(BIRMINGHAM).
Depots: Cheapside; Butlin Street 7; Tyseley.

5E ASTON CROSS GROUP.
Depots: Dartmouth Street 6:   Caudle Transport;
Premier Transport (part).
222 Gravelly Lane, Erdington 26:   Bayliss Transport (part);
H.B. Clarke;
Premier Transport (part).
Lichfield Road, Aston: Albert Road Transport;
Alliance Motor Transport;
Premier Transport (part).
Salford Bridge, Tyburn Road 24:   (D)Barrack & Fenton;
(D)Seymour Bros;

At 1953: ASTON CROSS(BIRMINGHAM).
Depots: Dartmouth Street 6; Lichfield Road 6;
Erdington 24; Handsworth; Nuneaton.

6E TYBURN GROUP.
Depots: Tyburn Road 24:   **S. Green & Sons**;
J.C. Billington;
L.H. Gorton;
N.J. Grimley;
H.C.N. Transport;
Jennens Brothers Ltd (pt)
Jones & Mitchell;
Maddens Road Services;
A. J. Millerchip;
Schofield Transport;
South Birmingham
Transport;
Wainwright Bros;
R.J. Whittaker; J. Wild.
Tyburn Road 24:   Northern Motor Utilities.
Redditch; Lodge Road: E.B. Cousins;
Goulchers Motor Service;
Johns Transport;
Longbridge Transport;
Woods Transport.

At 1953 TYBURN (BIRMINGHAM).
Depots: Barn Street 5; Lancaster Street 4;
Tyburn Road 24; Redditch; Tamworth.

7E BIRMINGHAM PARCELS.

8E HOCKLEY GROUP.
Not listed 1953. To 11E WEST BROMWICH GROUP.
Depots: Sheepcote Street: E. Davis;
J. Davis;
Gairs Transport;
Kings Heath Transport;
E. O'Connor;
J. A. Wells.
107 Whitemore Street: J. Frampton;
(A)General Roadways;
L. Mitchell;
(G)Tills Transport;
Transport Economy;
Walker Road Transport;
(C)J. & H. Whittaker.

9E HAY MILLS GROUP.
Depots: Yardley, Amington Road:

George Road:
Tyseley, Rushey Lane.

Hall Green, York Road:

At 1953: HAY MILLS (BIRMINGHAM).
Depot: Washwood Heath Road 8.

Bayliss Haulage (part);
T.E. Weatherhogg.
Hurst & Payne.
John Morton & Son Ltd:
(F)Smart Transport;
(F)Talbot Serpell.
J. Bedworth;
Rutty & Hughes;
D.H. Wilson.

10E NUNEATON GROUP.
Not listed 1953.
Traffic: General and Tipping.
Trunks: Liverpool, London.
Depot: Tuttle Hill:
Tamworth; Amington Road:

West Midland Roadways.
B.B. Transport.

11E WEST BROMWICH GROUP.
Depots: Langley Green, Clay Lane:

Smethwick; Engine Street:

West Bromwich; 121 Spon Lane:

Union Street:

At 1953 Depots: Langley Green;
Smethwick; West Bromwich.

Holland Bros;
(B)London Scottish
    Transport.
H. Aston;
Davis Bros.
C.H. Blower;
J. Campbell;
R. Harrison;
Miles Motor Service.
(D)Beaumont Brothers;
(H)Giles & Bullen;
(D)O.K. Carrier Co.,
T. Wilkinson.

SHROPSHIRE & STAFFORDSHIRE DISTRICT.
20E-22E, 24E, 26E-31E.

20E WELLINGTON GROUP.
Transferred 1951 see 32G WELLINGTON GROUP.

21E WALSALL GROUP.
Depot: Bentley; Wolverhampton Road:
Traffic: General and Tipping.

Bloxwich; Sneyd Lane:

Darlaston; 11 Willenhall Street:

Also at 1953: Darlaston and Bentley, Walsall only.

T.S. Charnell; E. Dakin;
R. Dawes; J.T.Elwell, T. Glaze;
Nunn's Carriers; Pritchard;
West Midland Roadways.
J. Astbury; J. Craddock;
Everitt;
Wallington Heath Transport.
A.T. Hartshorne; E. Hartshorne;
Hickenbottom; T. Rushton.

22E WOLVERHAMPTON GROUP.
Depots: Bilston; Queen Street:

Wolverhampton; Ettingsall Road:

Jenner Street:

At 1953: Jenner Street; Steelhouse Lane and Moxley.

Jack Gill; Arthur Hughes;
Queen Street Motors.
C. & L. Transport; G. Swift;
S. Meredith.
Broad Street Garage;
Car Conveyances;
Colbournes; H.W. Fox;
Walter Hyde; Mac's;
Parkinson; E.A. Smith; Wrights.

23E SHREWSBURY GROUP.
Transferred 1951 see 31G SHREWSBURY & CENTRAL WALES GROUP.

24E KIDDERMINSTER GROUP.
Not listed 1953.
Depots: Brierley Hill; Cottage Street:

Kingswinford; Portway Garage:

Ludlow; Clee Hill:
Stone nr. Kidderminster:

H.W. Johnson;
A.C. Kendrick;
Norris & Jones;
W.E. Price;
Woodridge.
Cartwright & Paddock;
J.H.C. Transport;
Pensnett Transport;
G. Pickett; S.T. Priest;
G.A. Taylor; C.G. Whitehouse.
Clee Transport; G.B. Davies.
Talbot Transport; R. Dudley;
W. Postings.

26E STAFFORD GROUP.
Depots: Rugeley; Wolsey Road:

Stafford; 92 Rickerscote Road:
At 1953: STAFFORD (RUGELEY).
Depots: Rugeley; Stafford; Uttoxeter.

W.H. Brown; R.Gee & Son;
Trent Valley Transport.
Tilstones Transport.

27E DUDLEY GROUP.
Depot: Dudley, Tipton Road:

At 1953: Dudley; Wordsley; Stone (Kidderminster).

Bate Bros;
(D)Wm. Baxter;
Bruton's Motor Services;
T. Darby;
Dudley & Blowers
    Green Transport;
J. Fellowes; G.Foster;
Great Bridge
    Motor Transport;
D. Hyde; Jackson;
A.E. Masters.

28E BURSLEM GROUP.
Transferred From C North Western Division.
Depot: Hamil Road:

Crewe, Mill Street:
Underwood Lane:
Haslington. High Street:

At 1953: NORTH STAFFS (BURSLEM):
Burslem; Crewe; Longton; Rushton Spencer; Whitchurch.

Clowes & Smith;
North Staffs
(H)Bradshaws Transport.
Preece.
Hill.
Wm. Mulcaster; Black;
Northwich Transport;
Robson.

29E TUNSTALL GROUP.
Not listed 1953.
Depot: High Street:

Regent Garage:

B.C.P. (Beresford,
    Caddy & Pemberton).
Geo Webb.

30E STOKE GROUP.
Depots: Campbell Road,
Boothen Green Garage:
Trunks: London, Birmingham.

Fenton, Whielden Road:
Trunks: Liverpool, Manchester, Widnes.

At 1953: Stoke; Tunstall.

J. Kimberly.

Beckett Bros.

31E LONGTON GROUP.
Also at 1953.
Depot: Church Street: Longton Transport.

LEICESTER & NORTHAMPTONSHIRE DISTRICT. 40E-41E, 44E-48E.

40E NORTH LEICESTER GROUP.
Not listed 1953.
Trunks; London, Derby,
Northampton, Nottingham.
Depot: Barrow-on-Soar;

Warner Street:	J. Squires; Toone Bros.
Groby:	Fred Edlin; **S. Latham**;
	Melton Transport;
	R. Murphy; J.J. Thody.
Ibstock, New Garage:	Bircher Bros.

Leicester: 35 St. Michaels Avenue,
Melton Road:	Bircher Bros;
	A.W. Whetton.
Oxford Street:	Marshall Bros.
Loughborough; 6/8 Selbourne Road:	
	T.W. Annbel (part);
	Goodacre;
	Kinders Transport (part).
Syston:	Roberts & Brooks.

41E SOUTH LEICESTER GROUP.
Depots: Blaby; Lutterworth Road:
     Brindley;
     British Waste Transport;
     Howards Transport;
     Kinders Transport (part);
     Narborough Transport (pt);
     Sutcliffe Bros.
Corby; Gretton Road:
     Ketland Transport;
     Kettering Transport;
Weldon Corby-Bagshaw.
Leicester; 272 Harrison Road:
     Leicester Motor Haulage;
     Mackley Sharp Bros;
     W. & L.T. Shipman (part).
South Wigston; Park Road:
     A.B.C. Motor Carriers;
     A.M. Biddle;
     J. Bray;
     Pratts Transport; Statham.

At 1953: SOUTH LEICESTER(BLABY).
Depots: Blaby; Abbey Lane, Leicester;
Loughborough; Rugby; Weldon.

42E LEICESTER PARCELS.

43E NORTHANTS PARCELS.

44E LEICESTER TIPPING GROUP.
Depots: Glenfield, Dominion Road:
Stoney Stanton, Hinckley Road:
     Elliott; Lane & Peters.
at 1953 LEICESTER TIPPING (STONEY STANTON).

45E NORTHAMPTON GROUP.
Depots: South Bridge: Globe Transport Works
Traffic: General and Meat.
     A.W. Darby.
Stenson Street: C. & W.H. Butt; Norman Bell.
Stoney Stratford, London Road:
     Bramwell's Haulage;
     Samuel Reynolds.
At 1953 also at Bedford; Wellingborough.

46E LIVESTOCK GROUP.
Depots: Badby; Barford; Milverton;
Knowle & Dorridge Goods Station;
Wellington Street, Thame.   G.W. & L.S.M.R jnt;
     Oldham
At 1953 LIVESTOCK (MILVERTON, LEAMINGTON SPA).

47E LUTON GROUP.
Depots: Luton; Dunstable Road: **Parrott**; Kingsway;
     Bramhall;
     Phillips; (B)Carroll.
Leagrave Road: Lucas.
At 1953 LUTON/LEIGHTON BUZZARD(LUTON).
Depots: Aylesbury; Dunstable; Leighton Buzzard.

48E LEIGHTON BUZZARD GROUP.
Not listed 1953.
Depots: Grovebury Road: Biggs.
Stanbridge Road: Turney.

NOTTINGHAM & DERBY DISTRICT. 61E-66E; 68E-69E.

60E NOTTINGHAM PARCELS.

61E SOUTH NOTTINGHAM GROUP.
Traffic: General; Boots;
British Sugar Corp; B.P.B.
Depot: Iremonger Road, London Road: Cobden Transport; J. Evans;
     W.H.C. Ford; J. French;
     Hollowson Transport;
     (H) J.J. McVeigh;
     Robin Hood Transport.
Sub-depot: Parkyns Street,
Ruddington;   Dabell Bros; J.P. Middleton.
Bulwell, Hucknall Lane: Marshall.
At 1953 only at London Road.

62E DERBY GROUP.
Traffic: General, Qualcast (not Parcels).
Depots: Meadow Lane, Alveston: W. Allsop;
     Thomas R. Beason;
     Derby Motor Transport;
     Ilesley Bros;
     B. Keeling; E. Roper;
     Smith Haulage;
     Standard Transport;
     (C)Stevenson Transport.
89 Cameron Road, Derby: Mansfield & Dawson.
Riddings, Green Hill Lane: J. & G. Leah. H.J. Swan.
42 Pease Hill Road, Ripley: S.R. Abbott; J. & W. Melrose;
     Whiteman & Hawkins;
     Wright & Statham.
At 1953 only at Alveston and Melbourne.

63E NORTH NOTTINGHAM GROUP.
Traffic: General; Gotham & Co. Ltd;
Gypsum Mines; J.Player; Stanton Iron Works.
Depots: 37/55 The Wells Road,
Nottingham: **R. Keetch**; Advance Transport;
     Buttolph; Henson;
     Keetch & Sandells; Seaton;
     Wallis Transport.
Comery Avenue, Carlton Road;   W. Clarke; J. Keetch;
     J.A. Rankine
Hucknall Lane, Bulwell: A.R. Marshall.
At 1953 only Wells Road and Bullwell Depots.

64E SOUTH DERBYSHIRE GROUP.
Traffic: General and Tipping.
Depots: Burton-on-Trent,

Lichfield Road, Branston:	**West Midland Roadways**;
	W.T. Allen;
	L. Rodgers;
	Vale;
	Watson;
Hilton:	Dereham & Allen.
Melbourne, Blackwell Lane: Derby:	J.B. Laban.
Swadlincote, Midland Garage:	E. Ball;
	C.E.B. Transport;
	Harrison Transport;
	J.W. Johnson; F. Kirk;
	Osbourne; Transit Services;
	R.J. Shilton.
Uttoxeter, Dove Bank, Derby Road:	Baillies Transport;
	E. Pattison;
	P. Warburton.

At 1953 only Branston; Hilton; and Swadlincote Depots.

65E DUKERIES GROUP.
Depot: Chesterfield; Walton Road:
At 1951 transferred to 61D CHESTERFIELD GROUP

	Chesterfield Transport.
Mansfield, Carfax Garage,	
Chesterfield Road:	F.C. Ashton;
	J. Ball;
	J.E. Berney;
	Mansfield Haulage.
Nursery Street:	Scott

At 1953; DUCKERIES (MANSFIELD): Mansfield; Riddings.

66E NORTH DERBYSHIRE GROUP.
Depots: Ambergate, Ripley Road:
Trunk to connecting depots.

	(B)Cowan.
Darley Dale, Unity Garage:	**Toft Bros & Tomlinson**.

At 1953 also Harlington; Wirksworth.

68E SHERWOOD GROUP.
Traffic: General.

Depots: Worksop, Dock Road:	W. Fletcher;
	T. Hunt;
	Sergeants Transport;
Church Lane, New Ollerton:	C.J. Brammer;
	B.Fearn:
North Road, Retford:	J. Morris.

At 1953 transferred to 68D SHERWOOD (WORKSOP).

69E GAINSBOROUGH GROUP.
Depot: Dunham-on-Trent:
Traffic: General and Livestock.

	W.F. Cooper

At 1953 transferred to 68D SHERWOOD (WORKSOP).

80E OXFORD GROUP.
Transferred 1951 to 44G OXFORD GROUP.

81E DROITWICH GROUP.
Transferred 1951 to 47G DROITWICH GROUP.
Depot: Droitwich; Chapel Bridge:
Traffic: British Sugar; General;
Trunk, London.

	H.B. Everton.

82E WORCESTER GROUP
Transferred 1951 to 46G WORCESTER GROUP.

F. SOUTH WESTERN DIVISION
BOUNDARIES at 1949; Cornwall, Devon; Somerset; Wiltshire; Hants; Bristol, Isle of Wight, Berks (excl. portion east of line from Twyford to Blackwater).

BRISTOL DISTRICT 1F-7F.

1F CENTRAL BRISTOL GROUP.
Trunks: Plymouth, Birmingham, London.

Depots: Albert Road:	Dimond, Hawker;
	(C)North Western
	Transport Services;
28-30 Argyle Road:	**Smart Transport**.
Barton Hill:	Russett.
Hambrook:	F.A. Bayliss
Maze Street:	Ashley Down Transport.
Yate, Wester Road.	

Traffic: Tipping.
At 1953; Depots: Albert Road 2; Cheese Lane 2 and Unity Street 2; Bedminster.

2F EAST BRISTOL GROUP.

Depots: Days Road:	Jacobs; Pioneer.
Keynsham, Temple Street:	Carpenter Bros;
	J.T. Godfrey; Pope.

At 1953: Depot: Days Road.

3F SOUTH BRISTOL GROUP.
Depots: Bath Road:

Feeder Road:	Russett; Moorfields Transport;
	United Motorways.
Burnham-on-Sea:	H. Brown.
Weston-super-Mare:	R.E. Goodall;
	Dudd;
	Hodges; Pemberthy.
Yatton:	H.H. Reynolds.

4F BATH & WELLS GROUP.
Traffic: General; Tipping.
Depots: Bath,

Locksbrook Road Garage:	Charlish & Price;
	Guest Wood & Ling;
	R.T. Watson.
Lower Bristol Road:	The City Steam
	Transport Co.
Shepton Mallet, 10 Compton Road:	Oatley.
Evercreech, Weston Town:	Green.
Wells, Princes Road:	Willmott.

At 1953 BATH & WELLS (WELLS).
Depots; Bath; Wells.

5F TAUNTON & NORTH DEVON GROUP.
Traffic: General; Tipping. With 24F to become 81F.
At 1953 BRISTOL PARCELS.

Depot: Appledore, Bidna yard:	Lamey;
	Metherall.
Bridgwater, Bristol Road:	Fursland; W. Jones.
Burnham-on-Sea:	
12 Abington Street:	H. Brown.
Chumleigh,	Highlands; Parker.
Cullompton:	Whittons; Milton's.
Curry Rivel:	Osmond Bros.
Highbridge, Newtown Road:	Major.
Taunton, 27 High Street:	Bowerman.
Witheridge, High Street:	
Wivelscombe:	Pulsford's.
Barnstaple, WR Goods station.	

Traffic: Railway Cartage. | Chaplins.

6F SOUTH DEVON & CORNWALL GROUP.
Not listed 1953. Became 81F.
Depots: Bodmin, Burnards Lane: — G. J. Smith.
Kingsbridge: — W.G. Jarwood & Sons
Kingsteignton: — **Clarke & Brown.**
Newton Abbot, 24/6 Wolborough Street: — Frank White.
Perranporth: — Brewer.
Plymouth, Sutton Road: — Huxham; E. Baker.
SR Devonport Goods Station,
and WR Friary Station:
Traffic: Railway Cartage. — Chaplins.
St. Austell, 40 South Street: — N.E. May.
Tavistock, 3 Parkwood Road: — White & Goodman.
WR Goods Station:
Traffic: Railway Cartage. — Chaplins.

7F BRISTOL PARCELS.
At 1953 5F.

SOUTHAMPTON DISTRICT. 20F-27F.

20F POOLE & YEOVIL GROUP.
At 1953 POOLE/YEOVIL (POOLE).
Depots: Blandford,
Damory Court Street: — Cuff.
Handley, High Street: — Day.
Ilminster, 16 Ditton Street: — Patten.
Poole, The Quay: — Allen; Dacombe; Gillard; Nescroft.

West Shore Wharf:
Trunks to; London, Birmingham, Bristol.
— **Southern Roadways**; Southern Commercial Motors.
Sturminster Newton: — H.C. Turk
Yeovil: Woodlands: — Bird Bros.
S.R. Town Station:
Traffic: Railway Cartage. — Chaplins.

21F PARKSTONE GROUP.
Traffic; General; Tipping.
Trunk; Birmingham; London.
Depots: Fancy Road: — Heathfield; Pioneer.
Ringwood Road: — Clapcott; H. Curtis.

22F SOUTHAMPTON GROUP.
Traffic: General; Fruit; Tipping.
Depots: 20 Westwood Road: — Downer,
Canal Walk:
Traffic: Ships Stores; Local.
— Andrews.
Hampton Park Works: — Geo Baker, Andrews, Pitter.
Totton, Elling Lane: — Hatcher.
Millbrook, SR Goods Station:
Traffic: Railway Cartage. — Chaplins.
At 1953 also Chandlers Ford.

23F PORTSMOUTH GROUP.
Depots: Camber Quay: Dock Traffic.
Haslemere Road: — Parks of Portsmouth Ltd.
51 St. James Street:
Trunk to London.
— Taylor; Powerscourt Transport.
Fratton, SR Goods Station:
Traffic: Railway Cartage. — Chaplins.
Liss, Hill Brow: — Liss & District.
East Cosham, 25 Carlshalton Avenue:
— Hugman.
Southsea, 86 Belgrave Street: — **Byng.**

24F EXETER GROUP.
Not listed 1953. Became 80F
Traffic: General; Tipping.
Depots: Haven Road:
Traffic: General and Meat.
St. Thomas, Ferndale Road: — **Crews.**
Queens Road: — German Bros (part); East Devon Road Transport. German Bros (part).
Exmouth, The Parade:
Exeter Central Station:
Traffic: Railway Cartage. — Chaplins.

25F EASTLEIGH PARCELS.

26F ISLE OF WIGHT GROUP.
Depots: Cowes, Newport, Ryde;
Shanklin, Wooton, Yarmouth.

27F RAILWAY CARTAGE GROUP.
Depots: See under Chaplins in places served.

28F EXETER PARCELS.

READING DISTRICT. 40F-42F.

40F READING GROUP.
Depots: Cardiff Road: — **Talbot-Serpell.**
St. Mary's Butts:
Traffic; Railway Cartage.
— Chaplins.
Basingstoke, Mapledurwell: — **Hutton.**
Thatcham: — **T.R.T.S. (Thatcham Road Transport Service).**

41F SWINDON & SALISBURY GROUP.
Depots: Drove Road:
Traffic General and Meat,
Trunks to London, Bristol.
— **Swindon Transport**; Bradley's Carriers; Mattingley; Okus Quarries.
Devizes, New Park Street: — Judweeks.
Pewsey: — G. Plank & Co.
Salisbury, Brown Street;
Trunk to London. — Mould.
West Harnham: — **John Lampard.**
Milford SR Goods Station:
Traffic: Railway Cartage.
— Chaplins.

42F MELKSHAM/FROME GROUP.
Traffic: Tipping, Trunks to London, Bristol, Manchester, Newcastle.
Depots: Melksham,
New Broughton Road: — Crook.
Spa Road:
Traffic: General, Meat; Tipping.
— W.A. & A.G. Spiers.
Frome, Chantry: — **Evemy.**
Bradford-on-Avon,
Frome Road Garage: — Black & White Transport.
Bratton, Lower Road: — Pearce.
Bruton, Patwell: — Viney.
Gillingham, Shaftesbury Road: — **Hine.**
Henstridge, Shaftesbury Road: — Sealey.
Warminster, The Old Brewery: — Evemy; White.

Following the reorganistions to divisions at 1953 the new groups or depots were:

43F GUILDFORD
Depots: Bracknell, Dorking, Guildford, Horsham.

The HOME COUNTIES DISTRICT. 60F-64F.
Was transferred from South Eastern District

60F EAST KENT (CANTERBURY).
Formerly 1A.
Depots: Canterbury; Deal;
Faversham;
Folkestone; Minster.

61F MID KENT (MAIDSTONE).
Formerly 2A.
Depots: Larkfield;
Maidstone,
Marden; Tonbridge.

62F MEDWAY (STROOD).
 Formerly 4A.
Depots; Rochester;
Sherness;
Crescent Street,
also London Road, Sittingbourne;
Strood; Swanley

63F ROTHER VALLEY (TENTERDEN).
Formerly 8A.
Depots; Ashford;
Battle;
Headcorn; Rye;
Tenterden.

64F BRIGHTON.
Formerly 20A.
Depots: Brighton;
Haywards Heath;
Shoreham; Uckfield.

80F EXETER GROUP.
Formerly 24F.
Depots: Exeter;
Sidmouth.

81F TAUNTON & NORTH DEVON (TAUNTON).
Formerly 5F and 24F.
Depots: Appledore; Barnstable;
Bridgwater; Chumleigh;
Cullompton; Highbridge;
South Molton;Taunton;
Watchet; Wheddon Cross;
Wivelscombe.

82F SOUTH DEVON & CORNWALL (NEWTON ABBOT).
Formerly 6F.
Depots: Bodmin; Kingsbridge;
Newton Abbot; Plymouth;
St. Austell; Tavistock.

83F EXETER PARCELS.

G. WESTERN DIVISION
Covers all Wales except Anglesey. North Cearnarvon and Denbigh, Herefordshire and most of Gloucestershire, and Oxfordshire, South Worcestershire, South Warwickshire, North Berkshire and extreme North Wales.

SOUTH WALES DISTRICT. 1G-2G, 20G-21G.

1G NEWPORT GROUP.
Traffic: General; Tipping. Trunks London, Gloucester, Liverpool, Luton, South and West Wales, and E Divn.

Depots: 74 Alexandra Road:	Elliotts Transport; Granville.
Clayton Street:	Gibsons Road Transport;
	Summers Transport.
Dock Street: 22.	All British Carriers; Lewis.
Chepstow, Larkfield Garage:	Ward.
Pontypool,	Turnpike:
Rogerstone:	Russell.

2G CARDIFF GROUP.
Traffic: Trunks; London, Gloucester, Lancashire, South and West Wales.

Depots: Brunswick Street:	Sparks; Tuckers;
	Wynns (Some).
East Canal Wharf:	Lansdowne; Andrews; Lees.
Newport Road;	All British Carriers;
	(A)General Roadways.
Barry, Cadoxton:	Thomas.
Grangetown, Old Shipways/Shipyard:	
	Andrews.
Dinas Powis:	
Traffic: General and Livestock.	
	Hills.
Merthyr, 1 Chart Street:	
Rumney, Downton Garage:	Price.

20G SWANSEA GROUP.

Depot: Broad Quay:	Sendus Anywhere
Paxton Street:	Laugharne Morgan;
	Jacksons; Jeffrey.
Gorseinon, West Street:	Bowen.
Gowerton, Church Street:	Galey.
Landore, Cwmin Terrace:	Corkers; Hayes;
	South Wales Roadways;
	A. Trott.
Morriston, 109 Chase Road:	W.J. Davies; Seaman.
Pontardulais:	Davies.
Skewen, Lonlas Yard:	All British Carriers.

21G WEST WALES GROUP.

Depots: Neyland, Victoria Garage:	West Wales Roadways.
Pembroke, The Quay:	West Wales Roadways.
Tregaron, Llangei House, Caernarvon:	Bland.

SHREWSBURY & WEST WALES DISTRICT. 30G-32G, 42G.

30G WREXHAM/WELSHPOOL GROUP.
Traffic: General; Livestock.

Depots: Newtown,	
Clifton Transport Garage, New Road:	Bayley.
Wrexham, Berse:	Ombler Bros; Bell.
Welshpool, Vulcan Works, Salop Road:	
Trunks: London, Birmingham, Bristol,	
Liverpool, Manchester.	
	Aber Carriers.

31G SHREWSBURY GROUP.

Depots; Shrewsbury,
Spring Gardens: Shrewsbury Transport.
Ditherington:
Gobowen: Direct Transport;
                                    S. Burgess; Jones Bros;
                                    L.H. Owen.

Minsterley: Lewis Brothers (Haulage) Ltd;
                                    W.F. Jones; W.E. Lewis;
                                    F.T. Payne.
Newton, New Road: Gwyn Boyle.
Whitchurch, Highgate: Denmans, Gleave;
                                    S. & M.W. Transport.

To 28E Burslem, 1953.

32G WELLINGTON GROUP.

Depots: Dawley; Heath Hill: N.S. Arden; C.R.T. Jones;
                                    H.A.L. Price; F. Rawson.
Donington;   E. Hemmings; W.E. Hitchen.
Newport; Weston Jones: Clowes.
Forth Road: Newport Transport.
Shifnal; Broadway Garage: S.J.G. Atkins & Son;
                                    E. Clowes: A.J. Price.
Wellington;   Lawley Furnaces; C.R.T. Jones.
Watling Street: Chetwoods; J.H. Ferrington;
                                    R. Hodkinson; J.T. Stone.

*By 1951 Divisional Boundary changes caused
Oxford, Gloucester District to be tranferred
from E Division to G Division.*

40G FOREST OF DEAN GROUP.

Traffic: General; Tipping.
Depots: Lydney, Hill Street: Cecil; T.W. Thomas.
Mitcheldean, Merrin End Garage: Read.

41G GLOUCESTER GROUP.

Traffic: General, Livestock, Tipping.
Depots: Chequers Road,
Tipping Section: Morris.
India Road: All British Carriers;
                                    Stephens Transport.
Sharpness, Berkeley Market Place: Sharpness Transport Ltd.
Tewkesbury, 11 East Street: Warner.

42G HEREFORD GROUP.

Traffic: General; Tipping.
Depots: Edgar Street: Morgan Friend; Elewings;
                                    Powell, Tanner.
Leominster, Longmans Garage,
King Street: Longmans.
Lyonshall: Burgoyne.
Ross-on-Wye: Station Road: Llewellyn.
Whitchurch, Hillcrest Garage;   Williams.

44G OXFORD GROUP.

Depots: Mayfield Road:
Traffic: General. Trunk: London.
                                    Thame Haulage;
                                    Chas Scott's;
                                    A.E. Booty; Dixon;
                                    Humphris Hire;
                                    Rainbows; A.H. Rix (part);
                                    Wellers Road Service.
Banbury, Foundry Road: A. Clarke; B. Gilkes.
Hardwick Wharf,
Traffic: General; Northern Aluminium.
                                    Andys;

44G OXFORD GROUP (continued)

Banbury General Motors;   Welford.
Chipping Norton, 47 West Street: Johnston.
Shipton-on-Cherwell (Kidlington)
Mercury Garage: (A)Mileham.
Middle Barton: W. Howe.

45G COWLEY GROUP.

Chinnor, Oakley Road: Harding
Sub-depot:
Littlemore: Harding.
Goring: Alexandra Haulage Co.

46G WORCESTER GROUP.

Depots: Bromyard Road,
Graham Garage: **Bailey & Turner**;
                                    P.K. Matthews; Hastelow;
                                    Tansell; Weavers
41 Hylton Road: A.G. Taylor.
Bidford-on-Avon, Victoria Road: Moore Bros; Wood & Wilshaw.
Evesham, Avonside: F. Preece.
Avon Street:
Trunks: Birmingham, Potteries, Liverpool, Manchester.
                                    Davies & Brownlow.
Littleworth Street: J. Marriot; J.A. Marshall.
South Littleton: J. Haskins.

47G DROITWICH GROUP.

Depot: Droitwich, Chapel Bridge: H.B. Everton.

H.EASTERN DIVISION

BOUNDARIES at 1949: Norfolk, Suffolk, Cambridge,
Huntingdon, North Essex, parts of Hertfordshire, Bedfordshire
and Northamptonshire, part of South Nottinghamshire.

NORWICH DISTRICT. 1H-3H, 5H-10H.

1H NORWICH GROUP.

Traffic: Local; General; Trunk: London, Birmingham.
Depots: Hall Road: **Eastern Roadways;**
                                    Giles & Bullen; Hall.
Surlingham: Cushion.

2H IPSWICH GROUP.

Depots: London Road: East Anglian Transport
                                        Services(part);
                                    Blomfield & Jackson;
                                    Giles & Bullen.
961 Woodbridge Road: **Days Transport**; Deans;
                                    Orwell Transport.
Yoxford: East Anglian Transport
                                        Services (part).

3H NORTH NORFOLK GROUP.

Traffic: General; Livestock.
Depots: Cromer, West Street: Cromer Haulage;
                                    Sheringham Haulage (part).
Snettisham, Station Road: Hodge & Son.
Stalham: **Stalham Transport**.
Swaffham, Rookery Farm: Leonard Bros;
                                    Mallon & Grange.
Wells next the Sea, Quay Garage: **Grange**;
                                    Sheringham Haulage.(part).
Wroxham: Alanda Transport;
                                    W. Littleboy Jnr.

4H STOWMARKET GROUP.
Transferred from 8H
Depots: Stowmarket: — O.G. Barnards.
Sudbury: — H. Abbott;
A.A. Chinery;
H.H. Kemp & Sons;
H.J. & G.E. Thorpe
(Mendlesham).

5H BECCLES GROUP.
Depots: 78 Blyburgate: — A.W. Denney.
London Road: — Robinsons;
Ingate Garage Ltd.
Ditchingham: — Lambert & Sons.
Yoxford: — East Anglian Transport.

6H YARMOUTH GROUP.
Traffic: General; Timber.
Trunk to London.
Depots: Maincross Road: — **Toby Transport**;
Greg. Swanston.
76a Southtown Road: — Chateau & Co Ltd.
15/Bay 2 Herring Market: — Reece.
Gorleston: — F.C. Farrow;
Millichamp Brothers;
Swanston.
Lowestoft, Stanley Street: — B. & B.
Oulton Broad: — R.W. Guymer & Sons.

7H BURY St. EDMUNDS GROUP.
Depots: Station Hill: — Suffolk Road Transport.
Barrow, The Vean: — Banks - Smith
Haulage Co. Ltd.
Diss, Victoria Road: — Bartrum; J. Wyatt Jnr.
East Harling, Roudham: — Lawrence;
Bulk Haulage;
Riches; Sleigh Bros.
Great Barton: — Crossways
Shipdham: — Morfoot.

8H NORFOLK & SUFFOLK PARCELS.

9H BISHOPS STORTFORD GROUP
Later to become 25H
Depots: 41 Dane Street: — F.G. Cotton & Sons.
75/89 South Street: — **Airlandwater**;
H.S. Jennings.
Stanstead Road: — Eastern Roadways.

10H FORDHAM GROUP.
Later to become 26H
Depots: Ely — Drake
Fordham: — H. A. Newport Ltd;
Bulk Haulage Ltd;
Collen & Reader.
Six Mile Bottom: — F.W. Barton.
Soham: — Alfred Griggs.
Southery:

PETERBOROUGH DISTRICT.
20H-24H & 27H.

20H HUNTS & ISLE OF ELY GROUP.
Depots: Ely, 51 Station Road: — Drake.
Littleport: — J.R. Halsall.
March, Creek Road: — Wilkinsons (March) Ltd.

20H HUNTS & ISLE OF ELY GROUP (continued)
March, Creek Road (cont); — F. Darby & Sons Ltd. (part).
Ramsey, Bury Road: — **Greenwoods**;
F. Darby & Sons Ltd. (part).
Sub-depot: St. Ives, North Road: — Everdell Bros.
Sutton, The Brook: — Fred Darby & Sons (part).
Swavesey: — Prime Godfrey Ltd.

21H PETERBOROUGH GROUP.
Traffic: General; Trunk; London.
Depots: Fengate: — Airlandwater.
Stone Lane: — Reads of Peterborough;
76 Fengate: — Granges Transport.
Wood Street: — B. & G. Transport;
Christmas;
Coles Bros;
Mason;
Meadows.
Ailsworth: — Taylor Bros (Haulage) Ltd.
Crowland: — Mason & Sons.
Deeping St. James: — F.H. Allen.
Easton: — Goe.
H.C. Hind Ltd;
C. & L. Transport.
Whittlesey, 17 Inhams Road: —
Watson;
Franks Bros.
Hurry Transport.
Peterborough Road: — Palmer.
Yaxley, Cross Roads Garage: — Peterborough
& Boston Transport.

22H WISBECH GROUP.
Traffic: General; Livestock.
Depots: Cromwell Road: — **H. W. Jones**;
E.E. Burton;
Southery Transport
Service Ltd.
Harecroft Road: — Rome Bros.
Guyhirn: — Bretts Transport.
Holbeach; Fen Road; — Edward Coward.
Holbeach; North Parade: — J. & E. Fletcher.
Leverington Common: — C.J. Tribe.
Upwell, 12/13 The Crescent: — Hardy.
Whaplode: — Almond Motors;
J.H. Fletcher.

23H CAMBRIDGE GROUP.
Depots: Cherryhinton Road: — Moss.
Ditton Walk: — T. & W. T. Stepney Ltd.
Gloucester Street: — M. Dickerson.
Newmarket Road: — H. Webb;
W.M. Nightingale.
Foxton: — **Welch's**.
Haslingfield: — Wisbey.
Biggleswade, Langford: — Laman.
Royston, North Road Garage: — Goddard & Dellar.
Melbourn: — D.A. Elbourne.
(Elbourne of Melbourne)
Stevenage, Newtown: — Bootman & Co; Trussell.

24H KINGS LYNN GROUP.
Depot: Alexandra Road: — Eastern Roadways;
Littleboys (part).
Estuary Road: — Littleboys (part);
Mitchley & Auker;
V.H. Waldon.
North Everard Street: — Giles & Bullen.
West Lynn: — Clifford Ebbs.
Terrington St.Clement: — P.C.H. Johnson;
Reliance Transport.

25H
Transferred from 9H Bishops Stortford.

26H
Transferred from 10H Fordham Group.

27H SOUTH LINCOLNSHIRE GROUP.
Traffic: General; Tipping.
Depots: Willoughby Road:
Gosberton Risegate, The Duke of York:

	C.Leslie Bates.
Pointon,	**T Leslie Bates & Sons (Haulage) Ltd.**
Spalding:	C.N. Banks Ltd; **Dodsons;** Grounds Transport; Potter's.
Whaplode:	Almond Motors.
West Pinchbeck:	E.M. Cole.

LINCOLN DISTRICT. 40H–47H

40H GRIMSBY GROUP.
Trunks to London, Birmingham, Lincoln, Notttingham, Sheffield.
Depots: Convamore Road:

	Blackburn; Goldthorpe; **Mcveigh;** Grimsby Roadways; Marshall; Ormond's.
22 Julian Street:	**Parrotts;** Carr.

41H LOUTH GROUP.
Depot: 22 Nichol Hill:

	Jaines.
158, Eastgate:	East Lincs Haulage Ltd. (part)

42H GAINSBOROUGH GROUP.
Traffic: General; Trunk, London.
Depots: Wembley Street:

	Bradshaw; Cousins; R.H. Wild.
Blyton, Laughton Road:	A.C. Clixby & Son; Clixby.
Kirton-in-Lindsay:	Herbert Grant.

43H BOSTON GROUP.
Traffic: General, Livestock.
Depots: 1 Mill Hill:

	S.T. Belton; Boston Haulage Co; The Holt Haulage Co.
Spilsby Road:	Thompson.
Hibberts Bridge:	Zealand.
Wrangle;	George H. Kime.
Brigg, Hibaldston:	J. Kirk; George Campion Evison.
Skegness, 49 Church Lane:	H. & A. Swift Ltd.
Spilsby, Hundleby, Mill Yard:	Hudson & Spence, (C)McVeigh.
Wyberton, London Road, Pincushion Garage:	
Broadsides Garage;	Pearson.

44H LINCOLNSHIRE GROUP.
Depots: Boston, Marsh Lane:

	Thomas E. Dabbs.
Bourne, Meadowgate:	Whatton's.
Woodhall Spa:	Roses Haulage.
Old Leake:	E.F. Kime.

45H LINCOLN CITY GROUP.
Depots: Brayford:

	F.W. Barlow; Denby; Hackford Porter; M.P. Transport (Lincoln) Ltd.
Mill Road, The Grange:	Roberts.
Monks Road:	**Thackers & Saltergate Transport Ltd.**
Newark Road:	
Traffic: Livestock.	
	E.R. Wright & Sons (Bracebridge) Ltd; G.W. Walker (Nettleham) Ltd.
Billinghay:	F Wells & Sons.
Horncastle, Station Yard:	T.G. Bell & Sons.
North Kyme:	Barrowcliffe.
Sleaford, 86 Westgate:	Houlden's Transport (Sleaford) Ltd.

46H SCUNTHORPE GROUP.
Depots: 5 High Street:

	Harvey.
Lindum Place:	Conveymole.
Scotter Road:	Abletts.
74 Station Road, Tipping Unit:	T. Goy & Sons (Hauliers) Ltd.
Ashby, Scotter Road:	Peatfield.

47H BRIGG GROUP.
Depots: Bigby Road:

	Fergus Procter; Miller & Vickers; execs. of A. Miller.
Wraby Road:	Martin.
Bridge Street:	**Slater**.
Brittania Garage:	Watson.
Wressle:	Hair.

60H COLCHESTER GROUP.
Traffic: General; Livestock.
Trunks to London, Cardiff, Gloucester, Oxford.
Depots: Victoria Case,
North Station Yard:

	Days; Seaborne Bros; W.H. Sexton; L.H. Thomas.
Ardleigh, Bromley Road:	
Traffic: General and Agricultural.	
Boxted.	D.C. Geater.
Chelsford, Baddow Road:	Rand Bros.
Copford, London Road:	Randall's; Days; E.L. Dyke.
Maldon:	Beadle & Son.
Manningtree, Wix:	**Hooks**.
Marks Tey:	Randall's Roadways; W.J. Levett Ltd.
Sible Hedingham, Gibson's Yard:	Cousins.
Tiptree:	**Autos**.
Witham:	Rowleys (Witham) Ltd.

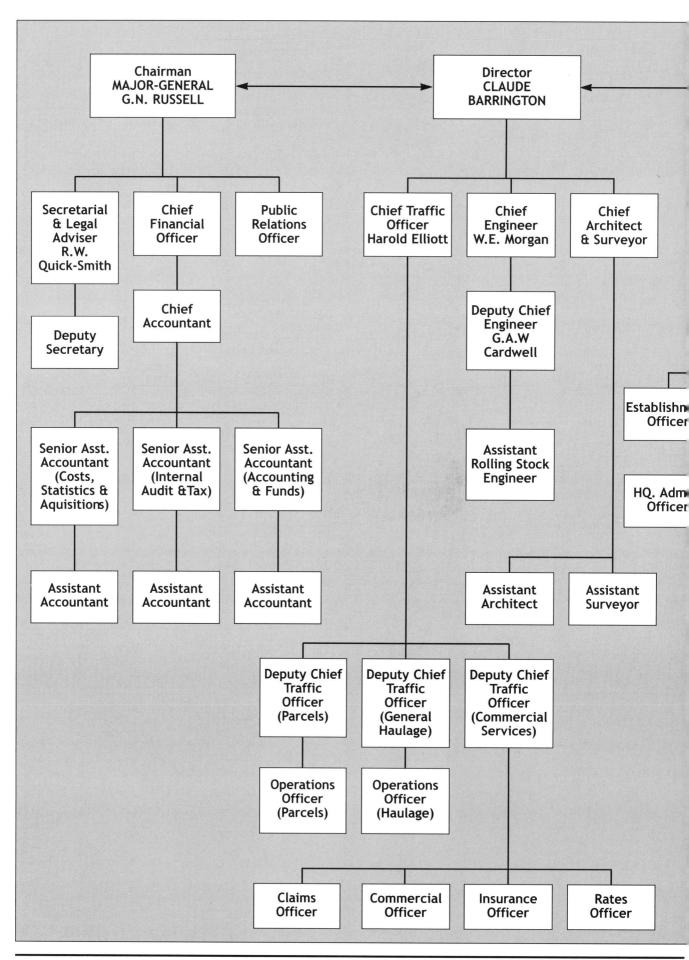

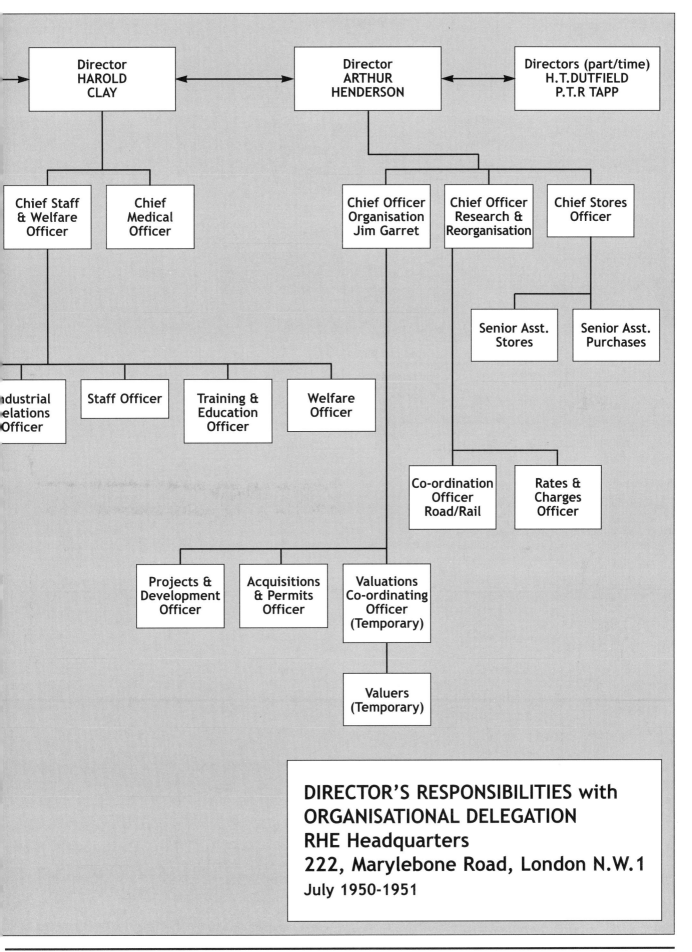

DIRECTOR'S RESPONSIBILITIES with ORGANISATIONAL DELEGATION
RHE Headquarters
222, Marylebone Road, London N.W.1
July 1950-1951

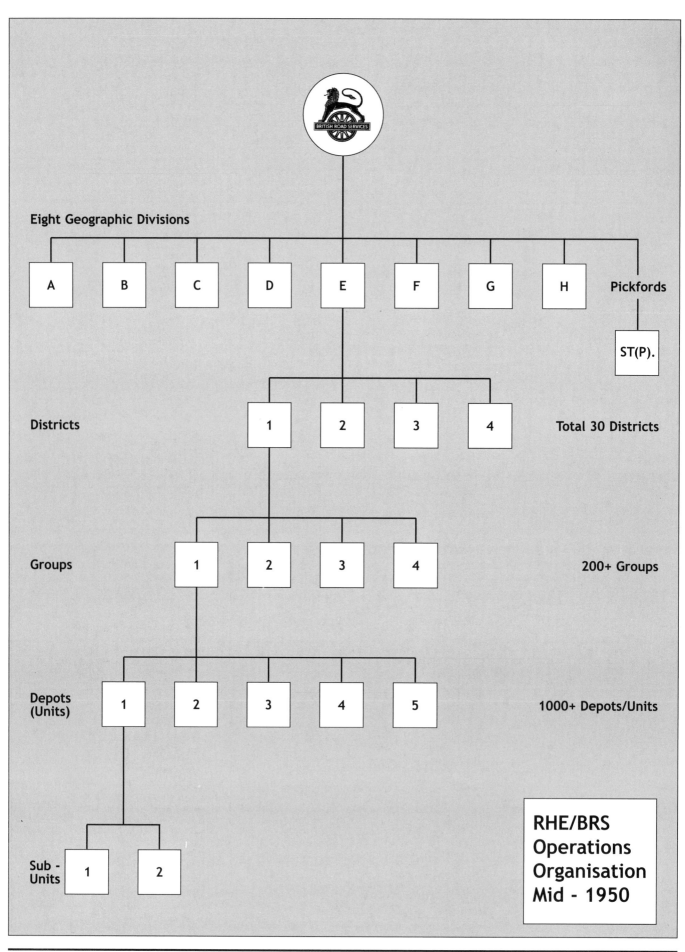

Eight Geographic Divisions

| A | B | C | D | E | F | G | H | Pickfords |

ST(P).

Districts — 1 2 3 4 — Total 30 Districts

Groups — 1 2 3 4 — 200+ Groups

Depots (Units) — 1 2 3 4 5 — 1000+ Depots/Units

Sub - Units — 1 2

RHE/BRS Operations Organisation Mid - 1950

Index

*Note: References to Illustrations, tables and
maps are highlighted in bold italics.*